PUSH

BREAKING THROUGH THE BARRIERS

I WAS CUT THREE TIMES, LOST 2.6 MILLION
DOLLARS IN NFL CONTRACTS AND BLEW OUT
MY KNEE.

THEN I BECAME AN OLYMPIAN FOR THE
UNITED STATES OF AMERICA.

JOHNNY QUINN

Made for Success
PUBLISHING

Made For Success Publishing
P.O. Box 1775 Issaquah, WA 98027
www.MadeForSuccessPublishing.com

Distributed by Made For Success Publishing

Library of Congress Cataloging-in-Publication data

Quinn, Johnny
Push: Breaking through the Barriers
p. cm.

ISBN: 9781613398869 (HDBK)
ISBN: 9781641462990 (eBOOK)
LCCN: 2017905989

CONTENTS

Let's connect on your favorite social media platform:

@JohnnyQuinnUSA

There have been three people to play in the NFL and compete in the Winter Olympics. The first two were Herschel Walker and Jeremy Bloom. I am fortunate enough to be the third. When it comes to the common query, "Is this book really different than all the other books out there?" Well, there could only be three versions of this book: a version from Herschel, a version from Jeremy, and a version from myself. At the time of this writing, Herschel doesn't have a book published, and Jeremy has a fantastic book out which primarily focuses on business principles. Therefore, I feel my book is one of a kind.

I have written down my journey in story form: a story to inspire and encourage you to PUSH and set audacious goals. To be clear, this is not a book on leadership, management, or productivity in the traditional sense. The truth is I haven't failed enough (yet) to write in depth on those topics. I'm thirty-two years old and, as a young leader, I need to fail more. I need more proverbial notches on my belt, if you will. I need more lessons on how to bounce back and how to face and fight adversity before I tackle those subjects in greater depth.

From cover to cover you will find foundational truths in all the top categories: leadership, management, relationships, productivity — you name it. How can this book provide all of those things? Well, young as I am, I had lost three jobs by my late twenties. I had lost $2.6 million and suffered through four surgeries — one as a result of a career-ending injury. I was left scared, confused, and not really sure what life had in store for me. Little did I know (leadership lesson!) that my failures, or what I like to call *temporary roadblocks*, were preparing me for what was to come next! If you had told me growing up in Texas that I would end up becoming an Olympic bobsledder for the United States I would have said, "You are crazy!" I couldn't see that next peak when I was going through the valley of the struggle, but when I finally made it through to the other side, I was able to see the peak clearly again.

If you struggle with anything, I wrote this book for you. If you've had your heart broken and need to PUSH again, this book is for you. I don't know what you're going through, but I'll let you in on a secret: the rewards at the end will be so much greater than the struggle, even if you're right in the messy middle, so don't give up. The fight is worth it. I promise.

Meet you at the starting block,

Johnny Quinn, U.S. Olympian

*To my wife... You are the woman of my dreams.
Your love and support are incredible.*

*To my parents... You were the first to believe in me. You
provided a loving home to go after my dreams.*

*To my brother... You were the better athlete of the family.
I always wanted to set the bar high for you.*

*To my teammates... You are the reason I laid it on the
line. We created a bond that will last forever.*

CHAPTER 1

STUCK IN A BATHROOM

"American bobsledder Johnny Quinn is the Olympics'
version of the Incredible Hulk. Or something like that."

— CNN

IT'S 60 DEGREES outside, which is warm for the Winter Olympics. My emotions and adrenaline are working overtime after walking in opening ceremonies last night. It took seven hours to get ready to walk into Fisht (Russian) Olympic Stadium with Team USA and all the countries around the world. I can't explain the feeling of wearing Red, White, and Blue and hearing, "Welcome, The United States of America!"

Unfortunately, we have 16 days before the 4-man bobsled competition. The experts in charge of building the Olympic schedule put the bobsled event at the end of the Olympics. It's going to be a challenge in and of itself to keep it together and remain cool during this two-and-a-half week break before we find out who can slide the fastest down an icy mountain track. Yes, we will have practice and training runs leading up to race day, but after last night's opening ceremony and the adrenaline rush, I am ready to compete on Olympic Ice.

This is when it hits me — I am back to reality, and the stupid bathroom door won't open. I have been taking a shower and daydreaming amid the emotions from last night's opening ceremonies and what it's going to be like on race day. I can picture our team winning the gold for the USA, but I can't seem to get my bathroom door open. I check the lock and the symbol points to unlocked. My team has an interview with the *Today Show* in a few hours, so I'm not pressed for time, but I am also not a fan of being locked in a bathroom — especially without a towel. I start twisting the doorknob back and forth to see if I can shift the door and unlock it. Nothing works. I move over to the hinges, observing like a master technician to see if they are loose or if I can take the hinges off. I wish I paid more attention in woodshop class. I bet we went over what to do when a door is stuck, but I can't recall any directions from my shop teacher.

Where is my roommate? Oh yeah, he has been lifting weights all morning. I bet he is letting off steam from opening ceremonies in the weight room. Growing increasingly frustrated, I start banging on the wall of the bathroom to see if I can alert my other teammates who's rooms are located across the hall from me. Maybe they'll somehow hear me and help with my jammed door. I create noise by hitting the side of the shower with the side of my fist. I continue to hit the side of the shower in constant succession, trying to create noise, but I receive no answer. I guess they can't hear me. Or if they can, they are letting me suffer and will hopefully come to my rescue soon.

I wish at that moment that I had my cell phone. I know exactly where it is: it's plugged in on the charger right on the other side of this bathroom wall. I think I took 100 pictures last night and the process of uploading all the pictures to social media must have drained my battery.

Surely, someone can hear me. In the Olympic village, part of our bathroom runs parallel to a hallway; maybe someone is walking to their room. I begin banging on everything I can find in the bathroom that could potentially make enough noise to notify someone. But my energy is wasted. Nothing works! No one comes to help.

I go back to the door and hit it hard out of frustration. To my shock, the door cracks, caving in right at the spot where my fist landed. I look at the door, perplexed; *I barely hit the door and yet it cracked!?* Now, this is interesting. What to do next? Well, naturally, I wind my arm up and hit the door even harder to see if it will happen again — and sure enough, my fist goes right through the door, making a hole. I can see the light coming in from our room. Freedom isn't that far away. I can't believe I just put my fist through a door. I wait for a minute or two and call for help again, but nobody answers.

You know what? I think to myself, *What if I make a big enough hole to reach my arm through and see if I can open the door from the doorknob on the outside?* I shift my arm through the hole and grab the doorknob, but it makes no difference — the door is still stuck. I can't open the door, even by turning the doorknob from the outside. You have got to be kidding me.

At this point, I have been stuck inside my bathroom for over an hour. I still have time to spare before our live interview with the *Today Show*, so I'm not in panic mode, or at least not yet. The damage to the door has already been done, so I decide I might as well use my fist as a hammer and make an even bigger hole to crawl through. I eyeball the measurement and calculate that three feet wide will be wide enough for me to wiggle my body through the hole to safety.

I crawl out of the battered door, avoid the door pieces on the ground and get dressed. My adrenaline is still pumping, but now for a different reason. *I can't believe I got stuck in my bathroom*, I whisper to myself to stay calm.

Why didn't my teammates come to help? Surely they heard me banging on the side of the shower. I got dressed and got ready to head out, but before I left, I looked back at the bathroom door — or what used to be the bathroom door. I stared in utter amazement at this giant man-made hole with door shrapnel lying all over the ground! Seeing the door completely busted open, I thought, *Uh-Oh! I am going to get in trouble for this!*

I took a picture on my phone and headed down to the Team USA office to notify our staff of the minor issue I ran into while taking a shower. I wanted to make sure I followed proper protocol in notifying our staff and making sure I squashed the idea of "horseplay" regarding how the door was broken. I wanted to clearly communicate that I was taking a shower and for whatever reason, the door got stuck and I had no choice but to break it down. To this day no one knows what happened — one thought is that since the Olympic Village was new, maybe the steam from the shower expanded the door in the frame.

The United States Olympic Committee (USOC) notified the Russian service staff of my issue with the bathroom door and a crew of three people immediately headed to my Olympic Village room to replace the busted door. It turns out they couldn't open the remaining portion of the door, and one of the service guys actually had to climb back through the man hole to get inside the bathroom. The service crew ended up busting down the rest of the door before replacing it with a new one. As much of a bond as the door and I had, it was good to see that the door was truly stuck and there was no way out besides busting it down.

As the service crew sized, fitted and installed our new door, I headed down to the trainers to get some treatment on my hamstring. Looking at my watch, I had an hour or so before our live interview with the *Today Show*. I was getting ultrasound treatment on my hamstring and looking at the picture of the busted door on my phone, thinking to myself, *What a funny scenario I was just in. I am at the Olympics, the day after opening ceremonies, and I get stuck in my bathroom. I am going to post this picture on social media! Who knows, maybe I will get a couple funny comments and see the humor in it, now that I've safely busted through a bathroom door.*

"I was taking a shower and the door got locked/jammed. With no phone to call for help, I used my bobsled push training to break out. #SochiJailBreak"

I put my phone down and rest my eyes as the ultrasound on my hamstring finishes up. I am still trying to process the events that have taken place over the last 24 hours. Opening ceremonies, locked in a bathroom, seriously trapped behind a bathroom door. This is too funny. I can't believe I had to bust down a door. I hear the sound of the ultrasound machine go off, signaling my time is complete, and I pick up my phone. Why does my phone feel hot? I look at the notification screen and it is going bananas! The phone battery has been working overtime during my session, and is literally hot to the touch. I swipe to open my phone, and laid eyes on something unlike anything I had ever seen before: the picture of the busted bathroom door has gone viral. The BBC is first to pick up the news; Yahoo grabs it next, and then other outlets around the world. Every news station or website is talking about this busted door. It has over 27,000 retweets, and has been seen by an estimated 10 million people around the world. Olympians from other countries are stopping me in the cafeteria so we can take a picture together. My Olympic Games have changed forever. I am now known as "the bobsledder at the Olympics who had to bust down the bathroom door..."

CHAPTER 2

KARATE KID

"Courage doesn't always roar. Sometimes courage is the quiet voice at the end of the day saying, 'I will try again tomorrow.'"

– Mary Anne Radmacher

HERE I AM, in the middle of the street, showing off my new moves. I start off with an impressive roundhouse kick, sweeping the leg into the air before a throng of curious onlookers. I'm dressed in white, decked out in full karate gear. Even at five, I realize that it's important to look the part. So I'm dressed to the nines, standing in my family's cul-de-sac in Westminster, Colorado, demonstrating firsthand to all the neighborhood kids that I will be the next Karate Kid.

Fast-forward about thirty minutes: dinnertime is right around the corner, and I know it's time to wrap things up for the day. I have to finish my karate demonstration strong. I go for the final kick — a full round-house to impress all of my friends who have now crowded around me for the performance. But then, something surprising happens. I miss the full turn and hit the cement pavement full-on, landing on my chin with my tongue serving as a mouthpiece between my upper and lower jaw. Ouch! My teeth go right through my tongue, but the pain hasn't fully set in just yet because of the dominance of my young pride. I can't tell what feels worse: the embarrassment at having failed my final karate act of the night in front of all the neighborhood kids, or the shooting pain that is quickly setting into my face.

I get up and try to brush off my failed karate display, assuring the other kids that it was a simple mistake that I will conquer for tomorrow's karate session. As I'm talking, I can feel the blood start to pour out from the gash on my tongue. I look down to see that it is now staining both my super cool karate uniform and the pavement below. I watch as my neighborhood friends' eyes become the size of saucers. The reality of what's happened is now starting to hit me, and I realize I have something seriously wrong with my mouth. The pain surpasses my embarrassment and tears begin to well up in my eyes. Without saying goodbye, I make a mad dash back to my house at the bottom of the cul-de-sac, holding my jaw with one hand and trying to catch the dripping blood from my tongue in the other hand. I get to the house, bust through the door and find my dad.

Now, I need to give you a little inside information on my dad. He is notorious for not knowing where my brother and I are throughout the day, and has ignored countless dissertations from my mom on how irresponsible he is for not watching us more closely while she is at work. He can see the blood in my hand and all over my fingers as I stand there, holding my mouth shut to control the pain, or at least I think that's the best way to control the pain. We rush to the emergency room and quickly find out I have a hole, the diameter of a pinky finger, splitting right through the middle of my tongue. Yes, you read that right. When I landed on the concrete, my teeth pierced all the way through my tongue. The nurse was able to control the bleeding, and the doctor came in to inspect my nearly severed tongue. Little did I know the doctor wasn't going to be able to repair the hole in my tongue with stitches; rather, I was going to have to give it time to heal on its own.

The next day at school, so many people were staring at me that I started to feel like a circus animal. I wasn't sure if they were discussing my karate performance (or lack thereof), or if everyone just wanted to see the hole in my tongue. It was great though. I felt as though I was back in control of a performance and could show off for my friends and impress everyone around me. However, this time, it had to do with a hole in my tongue rather than my karate skills. After receiving praise from all the boys and nasty looks from all the girls, I felt like one tough cookie. It finally settled in my mind that it was a poor decision to do karate on concrete. Next time I had better do karate on a mat.

That incident wasn't the only one that would happen that year; in fact, the year before first grade turned out to be a rough one for me physically. On top of almost sawing off my tongue, I had to get stitches in my head after a soccer tournament when everyone on the team celebrated by throwing soda cans up in the air after a victory! When you're five years old, you don't understand the law of gravity: what goes up must come down. Sure enough, a full soda can sent high into the air came down hard right on my head, nearly knocking me to the ground. That celebration required a trip to the doctor's office and eight stitches. Once again, I was the cool guy in class showing off my new battle wound to my friends. They thought it was so cool that I had blue stitches in my head. I think they may have even mistaken me for a superhero.

So you know how I said this was a tough year for me physically? Well, that same year, I also went on to break my arm. I was hanging on some monkey bars at a local park when I got the bright idea to climb on top of the bars and walk across them. If I were a betting man, I would guess my friends were probably there and I wanted to show just what I could accomplish to my group of kindergarten peers. But I didn't even make it past one bar; I slipped and fell to the ground immediately. I remember the feeling of sheer pain that shot up my left arm. It was something I had never felt before, and certainly not at that magnitude. My parents rushed me to the hospital for an immediate x-ray, and sure enough, I had broken the bone just above the growth plate in my elbow. Wow, that was a close call. So the doctor tells me I'll have to wear a cast, and I select a bright orange one for all of my friends to sign. That's three injuries and three doctor visits, and I am only five years old. My parents try to wrap their minds around the events that have taken place during my year as a kindergartener, and are a little concerned about what the future will hold for me and my body.

We found out shortly after that my future will be playing out in Texas, as my dad's work transferred him to the Dallas area. I will be starting first grade in McKinney, Texas, a suburb 30 miles north of Dallas. It's time to pack up and head to the state with cowboys and churches, or at least that is what the TV tells me about Texas.

CHAPTER 3

GOD AND THE GAME

*"I used to think you had to be special for God to use you,
but now I know you simply need to say yes."*

– Bob Goff

NO ONE RIDES a horse to work or searches the desert for water in a cactus — or at least not where we lived. I grew up in McKinney, Texas, which is a suburb 30 miles north of Dallas. We moved to McKinney when I was six years old, and from what I hear from the lifelong locals, McKinney is seen as a far and distant town from Dallas.

I have fond memories of growing up in Texas. The Dallas Cowboys were "America's Team," and it seemed as though every car and local business had the iconic Dallas Cowboys Star sticker, displaying their loyalty to the team. I didn't grow up a diehard Cowboys fan; I was more of a fairweather fan. But the weather was usually pretty fair in the early 1990's when my family first moved to Texas. At that time, the Cowboys were playing some really good football! They won a few Super Bowls with the big three: Troy Aikman, Emmitt Smith and Michael Irving. So whether you were a diehard fan or not, they were playing good football, and it was fun to watch.

Growing up watching football set in motion my dream of one day becoming a professional football player. I knew from a very young age that I wanted to play in the NFL. Every weekend, I would get so excited because

I knew what Saturday morning would bring: college football. I would sit there and watch as these young adults, who looked like grown men, would fly across my TV and display their athleticism, grit and toughness in order to score a touchdown and help their university win. I wanted to do that. I wanted to play in a big stadium, on television in front of thousands of fans screaming my name. I wanted to be the one sprinting down the sideline with the game on the line and the football in my hands. I wanted to hear the crowd erupt, chanting my name as I scored the game-winning touchdown.

As much as I loved all the college football I watched on Saturday, the pro football I watched on Sunday was even better! This was because Sunday was when the professionals would play football and showcase why they were the best of the best at what they did. I was particularly intrigued watching Jerry Rice, the greatest receiver to ever play the game. Some even say he's the greatest football player of all time. I really liked his style of play; he never dropped the football, he never complained, and he worked his tail off. The way he caught the football and ran after the catch, entering the end zone to help the San Francisco 49ers win the game, made a lasting impression on me. I knew I wanted to be just like him one day! I would watch SportsCenter and post-game interviews in the hopes that they would interview or talk about Jerry Rice. When they did, I would soak up all his knowledge and then demonstrate what I'd learned to my friends the next day when we'd play football after school on the practice field of Nora Haney Park. If I made a spectacular catch or scored a touchdown after jumping over a pothole, I would act the same way Jerry did on NFL Sundays. Just like Jerry, I would hand the ball back to my friend who was operating as the referee and line back up to go full speed on the next play. Because there were more touchdowns to be made and, just like Jerry, I wanted to score every single one of them.

I was such a Jerry Rice fan that I would mimic his every last move for my friends, including thanking God after making a great play. In fact, as I watched more football, I noticed that a lot of players would thank God in their post-game interviews. Many would also point to the sky when they scored a touchdown or made an impressive play, signaling to God. At first, I didn't know what they meant or what they were doing. But I knew that one day I wanted to become a professional football player, and that seemed to include acknowledging God after making great plays.

I grew up in a family that went to church and in a city and state that had no shortage of churches. Both then and now, there seemed to be a church at every corner of every street. The churches in Texas are almost like banks: they're everywhere. As you look at all the churches you begin to wonder if — just like the banks — do we really need that many? Are there that many people who will use all these banks? Are there that many people who will attend all these churches?

I came to find out fairly quickly that there were indeed many people who attended church, and that attending a service was a regular part of many peoples' Sunday schedule. Whether the person was an authentic Christ follower or not was up for debate, but many people could check church attendance off their list for the week. My earliest memory of going to church is of how fun the children's Bible classes were. We would play games, color and learn about a guy named Jesus who loved everyone. I thought that was pretty cool that Jesus loved everyone, because there were times that *I* didn't love everyone. For example: when the quarterback wouldn't throw me the football, or when my parents would make me turn off the TV after watching football for hours. At those times, I wasn't feeling the love. But to hear Jesus loved everyone and came to die for our sins so we could be right with God was awesome. At a young age, I accepted Jesus Christ as my personal savior and it was authentic; it was real. Looking back now, you could argue that since my parents believed in Jesus and made me and my brother go to church, it was just the natural thing for us to become Christians; after all, that's what our family did. But that's not the case. Because I was a child, my parents could make the decision for me to attend church. However, they could not make the decision for me to open my heart to Jesus; that was *my* decision to make.

Think about this same scenario as it might pertain to a child attending school. If I am a young child — say 6 to 7 years old — and I don't want to go to school, my parents are still going to take me. They aren't going to give me the choice of attending or not attending. But what kind of student I am, whether I study hard or slack off — that part is up to me. My parents can't determine what type of student I choose to be. They can encourage, demonstrate and share their experience with me, showing me why I would want to be a good student, but the choice is ultimately mine. So at 6 years old, when I am under the complete care of my parents, there is no choice about going to school and there is no choice about going to church. But the choice to accept Jesus as my Savior, just like the choice to become a good or bad student, was mine and mine alone. As you continue to read about my journey, what you will begin to see is how my perspective about life began to shift, how I started to drift through worldly success and how God's perfect plan and grace came to my rescue.

CHAPTER 4

THE YOUNG CHALLENGER

*"Today I will do what others won't, so tomorrow
I can accomplish what others can't."*

– Jerry Rice

ALL I WANTED to do was play sports — hockey, baseball, basketball, badminton, soccer, laser tag. You name it; I wanted to play it. Not only did I want to play a variety of sports, but I wanted to be the best at them. At that age, I had a healthy competitive spirit, or at least I think it was healthy. I wouldn't win and rub it in my opponent's face. I just simply wanted to win. And when I lost, I did not like the feeling. Therefore, I would try that much harder the next time we played the game to change the outcome and establish that winning feeling I grew to love so much.

As much as I loved football, my parents would not let me play organized football — or in other words, tackle football. My mom was afraid I would get hurt. She was an x-ray technician and was often on call when people would come into the emergency room after a serious accident. She didn't tell me this at the time, but I found out later on that some of the patients she had to x-ray would come into the ER in critical condition with life-threatening injuries. She would see people who had survived drunk driving or motorcycle accidents and were fighting to stay alive. For years, my mom would have to go into the hospital and x-ray these kinds of patients. I am pretty sure her fears of me playing tackle football related to the things she saw in the emergency room.

My dad grew up playing tennis and went on to play at a small school in Pennsylvania called Elizabethtown College. My mom didn't grow up playing sports, but my dad encouraged her to pick up a tennis racket from time to time and play with him. It turned out she enjoyed tennis, and my parents would often play couples matches together. So naturally, tennis was the first sport that I started playing.

I liked tennis. It was an exhausting workout that required speed, agility and hand-eye coordination. All that being said, it just didn't have the mesmerizing effect on me that football did. I continued to stay active in my early years by playing tennis, baseball and soccer. I loved playing a variety of sports, and I truly believe that versatility at such a young age helped develop my motor skills and overall athletic coordination. Those skills I learned early on could then be applied to any sport that I wanted to play and compete in down the road. Those sports were paving the road for me to play football.

I kept bugging my parents to let me play football. I begged and pleaded with them that if I was going to become a professional football player, then I had to start playing football. There was no other way to go pro! After countless times asking to play football, my mom finally caved in and made a deal with me. She said, "Once you get into 7th grade and football is part of the school program, you can go and try out." I couldn't believe what I was hearing. Was this the same x-ray technician that was just swearing off football days before? I was so excited because I could see the light at the end of the tunnel. I wanted to hit the fast-forward button to 7th grade so I could get my football pads and become one of the guys! It gave me new hope, and I was ready for 7th grade to get there as fast as possible.

In order to stay in playing shape and get ready for my 7th-grade football debut, I played a lot of pick-up football games at Nora Haney Park with my friends. We would all ride our bikes to the park after school and play touch football, which eventually turned into tackle football without any pads. Good thing Mom never found out about that. Maybe that is where my football skills began to develop — all the pick-up games and dodging potholes on the playground field.

Finally, the first day of 7th grade arrived, and it was time to get my football gear. I remember heading down to the locker room and noticing the putrid smell that hit my nostrils as soon as I walked through the door. It smelled like musty socks and dirty feet. I remember thinking *I sure hope my football pads don't smell like this, because I can't hold my breath for an entire game!*

The first day of 7th grade football tryouts went well. My pads fit, and it was awesome to wear a helmet. The only problem was that I was out of position. My middle school coaches who scouted out my class when I was in 6th grade pegged me as a quarterback. They felt that because of my speed and leadership ability (did I really demonstrate leadership ability in 6th grade?), becoming a quarterback and leading the team would be the best fit for me.

The first drill we learned as new quarterbacks was how to take a snap and hand the ball off. In other words, we learned a lot of boring stuff. I wanted action, and I wanted it now. I began to daydream about how successful Jerry Rice probably was in 7th grade as I looked over to see what the wide receivers were doing. Of course, they were learning the best route in the playbook: a deep fade. I continued to watch as the coach running the drill would bomb the football down the field for each receiver to catch. I stared in awe as the ball soared in the air only to come to a devastating halt on the grass as the new receivers missed the catch. I knew I was a receiver at heart. I mean come on; I watched all those films and interviews about Jerry Rice! I was destined to be a receiver. Plus, I had good hand-eye coordination. I knew that was where I wanted to be. I wanted to be a professional wide receiver football player.

I spent another day at the quarterback position to see if things would get better — and they didn't. I politely asked for a trade to the wide receivers, and without pushback from "management," my trade was accepted and I started to practice with the wide receivers! I immediately fell in love with the position, as I was good at running fast and catching the ball: two of the essential ingredients in becoming a successful wide receiver. I wanted coach to always send me on the deep routes so I could pluck the ball out of the sky and head to the end zone and help my team win. It didn't matter that it was only practice; I wanted to make sure I scored every time I touched the ball.

Middle school football was a ton of fun; I earned the starting wide receiver spot on the A-team and went on to be selected as wide receiver of the year for both 7th and 8th grade. Two years of middle school football gave me the confidence I needed once it was time to step on to the high school campus. I soon learned I was going to need that confidence, as there was another middle school that fed into our high school and they also had a really good receiver. He was tall and fast, and I knew it would be a battle for the starting position for the A-team freshman wide receiver spot. Challenge accepted!

CHAPTER 5

BIG DREAMS, BIG SACRIFICES

"The fears we don't face become our limits."

– Robin Sharma

FROM THE MOMENT I stepped onto my high school campus, the over-whelming feeling of not measuring up sunk in almost immediately. As an undersized freshman, I was intimidated by the upperclassmen and how big everyone else seemed to be. Despite this, my freshman year went pretty smoothly as I earned the starting wide receiver spot on the A-team and stayed busy playing basketball and baseball in the Winter and Spring. I went from feeling like I didn't measure up to enjoying that year.

It was during baseball season that I had an interesting after-school con-versation with the varsity track coach, Rod Washington. Washington, who was also the varsity running back coach, was a very successful sprinter in college. Anytime he would talk about speed, or demonstrate his speed tech-nique, I was keen to listen. I was finishing up some drills after school when I saw him walking over to me. I stopped what I was doing and said hello. I thought maybe he was just passing by, but no, he was there to talk to me about football. He said the varsity football coaches had been scouting the freshman team to see which upcoming sophomores might have the skills to play on varsity. He said that my name had been mentioned. I was so excited to hear that I was in contention to play varsity that I almost blacked out.

As a kid, I remember going to McKinney High School football games on Friday night and dreaming of the day I might be able to play varsity and wear the gold helmet. The gold helmet was reserved strictly for the varsity players. I told him I was going to work my tail off and be the best sophomore receiver I could be. Then the conversation went even deeper. Coach asked me what my long-term goals were and if I wanted to play in college one day. I told him that I wanted to go even further than college football and play in the NFL one day. Coach could see my eyes light up as I shared my dream with him. Much to my excitement, he responded enthusiastically and even had a game plan.

He said: "Johnny, you need to run track."

"Run track?" I asked, clearly confused.

"Yes," he said, "if you want to play in college and in the NFL, you have to be fast. You're fast now, but if you're serious about becoming a pro football player, you have to get faster. Much faster."

Something inside told me that Coach was right, that this was exactly what I needed to do. I needed to get faster, and it looked like track would help me accomplish that goal. While making the commitment to track and to increasing my speed would represent a new beginning for me, it also meant an ending: the ending of my baseball career. Baseball was in the Spring, and so was the track season. I would have to give up one for the other.

That was a real dilemma for me because I grew up playing baseball and was the starting centerfielder for the freshman team. I had this big, lofty goal that one day I would become a starting wide receiver and the starting center fielder on varsity for the McKinney Lions! But that was no longer a possibility. Still, it was a sacrifice I felt I needed to make to get myself in better shape for football. As much as I loved baseball, I loved football even more. I knew that all those years growing up and playing baseball were coming to an end. I loved playing football and the thought of playing professionally someday outweighed any disappointment about giving up baseball. Although this concept of running track was new to my football plan, everything coach Washington shared with me on the importance of speed and how track can translate to the football field made complete sense.

That day after practice, I remember sharing everything Coach said to me with my parents. I explained to them it was time to leave baseball and focus on track. One thing about my parents is they always encouraged my brother and me to dream big. There was never a dream that was too big. We never received feedback that our dreams were "cute," but we needed to be a little more realistic with what we wanted to do with our lives. If I came home and said I wanted to be an astronaut, my parents would help me find out exactly whom within NASA we needed to contact. If the next day I wanted to be the President of the United States, my parents would search for the contact information of our local congressman and start formulating a game plan. Because it was safe for my brother and I to dream big, the reality that only .08 percent of high school football players go on to play in the NFL never intimidated me. I knew that one day I would play in the NFL, and I had the support system in place to encourage me, push me and pick me up when I needed a boost!

CHAPTER 6

ALL EYES ON SOMEONE ELSE

*"The greatest pleasure in life, is doing the
things people say we cannot do."*

– Walter Bagehot

I GOT MY first taste of the scouting process when our high school star running back started drawing attention from the college scouts. Each week I'd see the scouts at our practice watching him intently, and I'd wonder what it would be like to be the person everyone was after. He signed with the University of Oklahoma after leading the state of Texas in rushing and winning Texas Gatorade Player of the Year. It was so impressive to see all these college scouts come to our practice. You better believe I was trying to make plays and showcase my skills while the scouts were in town. I knew the reason they were there was to see him, but I still wanted to see if I could catch a look or steal their attention. The experience of having them there served as a harrowing wake up call. I could feel the nerves set in as I came to the realization that next year, it would be signing day for my senior class — *and I wasn't currently getting recruited.*

My sophomore year I split time on junior varsity and varsity. It was so exhilarating being called up as a sophomore to wear the blue and gold school colors and run out of the tunnel on a Friday night. The only problem was I wasn't really playing much. Instead, I was riding the bench. My coaches wanted me to continue to develop, and as I grew into my body, they would rotate me in every week just to make sure I was getting some playing time. Sometimes that meant dropping back down to junior varsity. I started to worry that my football career wasn't developing the way that I had been hoping it would, and that if something didn't change soon, my NFL career might forever stay only a dream — not a reality. In my mind, I had this notion that in order to play in the NFL one day, you had to be a starter on varsity as a sophomore.

Unfortunately, my junior year wasn't starting out much better — at least from a production standpoint. We had such a good running back that it didn't make sense to throw the football all that much. We would hand it off, and he would do most of the work. For our running back it was great; it really gave him a chance to develop and show his skills. But for little ol' me, it wasn't so great. I wasn't getting the yardage and plays that I needed in order to get national attention. That being said, I still loved practicing during my junior year because scouts from Florida State, Notre Dame, Michigan, Texas, USC and every other big-time school would frequent our practice fields to catch a glimpse of our star running back. Each day in school I would daydream about the spectacular catch I would make in that afternoon's practice to capture the attention of the scouts and punch my ticket to a prestigious school and a playing career.

That year, we made it to the first round of the playoffs, and the game location was set at the Dallas Cowboy's stadium. Now I know what you're thinking. You're thinking of Jerry's World with the giant Jumbotron. But that's not where it was; that stadium hadn't been built yet. We were playing at the old Cowboy's stadium that has since been turned into a parking lot. Nevertheless, getting dressed in the Cowboys locker room and stepping out onto the field with the giant Cowboy star at the 50-yard line was a dream come true! The dream wasn't necessarily about the Dallas Cowboys, or that particular stadium, but about the prospect of playing my first football game on a professional football field. Finally, that had happened, and it was incredible. I remember looking into the stands at the very top of the stadium and imagining what it would be like to one day call myself a professional football player. Although we lost that game and had an early exit from the playoffs, the experience of being there and playing on that field reaffirmed that all my hard work was leading to something and that my ultimate goal of playing in the NFL one day could actually happen!

Nonetheless, I returned to school with the sobering reality that I was only a year away from my signing day, and was not in a good position in terms of being recruited. During my sophomore year, I only had one reception for six yards. During my junior year, my football stats were nine receptions for 96 yards. These statistics were awful: a ten-game season, and only nine receptions? That means on average I didn't even catch one pass per game. I had received no awards, no honors, and worst of all — no college interest. I knew God had a plan for my life, but I was starting to get a little confused and concerned as to how it was all going to pan out. College football scholarships go to productive high school football players and at that moment in time, I was not what you'd call *productive*... at all.

CHAPTER 7

COLLEGE RECRUITING WHIPLASH

"You must expect great things of yourself before you can do them."

– Michael Jordan

DURING MY FRESHMAN year of high school I played football, basketball, baseball and ran track. It was by trying different sports that I discovered that football was truly my passion. It was a blessing to learn this early on in my high school career as, once I realized what I loved most, I was able to focus on it strictly. My freshman, sophomore and junior years had really been interesting with regards to my recruiting journey. At the time, I did not know (or at least to the true extent) that sophomore year was when I really needed to be proactive in order to get my name out there. After limited playing time on the varsity team as a sophomore, and no letters or calls, I knew I was not on any scout's radar.

It really was not until after my junior year that I finally caught a break. That summer I attended a football camp at Texas Tech University. It turned out to be one of the best decisions that my family and I ever made. It was there that I had the opportunity to showcase my skills to the very people in charge of recruitment and stand out amongst hundreds of players. I performed well enough that I was selected to personally meet with the head coach at the time, Mike Leach. This is exactly what I needed. I now was on a college watch list, and on Texas Tech's radar.

By the time my senior year rolled around, I was excited that Texas Tech was showing interest and would be sending scouts to watch me play during the upcoming season. Remember, Texas Tech found me because I found them first! Still, as my senior season began, my family and I could not understand how some football players already had scholarships and had committed to universities. My mom's favorite words of encouragement during my entire recruiting process, which actually couldn't have been further from the truth, were: "If you are good enough, they will find you!"

My senior year went better than I could have even imagined. Let's just say a lot of footballs came my way and I worked my hardest to pluck each and every one of them out of the big, blue, Texas sky. Every week The Dallas Morning News published a list of area-receiving leaders, and each week my name was at the top. Double-digit receptions in multiple games gave me a comfortable lead in the Dallas/Fort Worth area, but I had no idea I was leading the entire state of Texas.

I soon faced a match-up against a nationally-ranked defensive back that played in my district. This top-ranked recruit had committed to the University of Oklahoma his junior year, and every college scouting service had him high on their recruiting boards. My family and I thought that if I won the battle against one of the top-ranked defensive backs in the nation — a player who had already committed to one of the top college football programs in the country — surely scouts would be knocking at my door, eager to have me attend their universities. I approached the game with great trepidation and great focus, but I shouldn't have worried; the game went far better than I could have hoped. I played as well as I had ever played and finished the night with four touchdowns, including the game-winner in overtime. After all of that game's excitement, I continued to play well during the season and increase my lead as the state leader in receptions. But much to my chagrin, nothing changed for me in the recruiting process. The level of interest from small schools remained the same, and Texas Tech continued to keep tabs on me from afar.

As a team, we had a mediocre year, finishing 5-5 and missing the play-offs. Fortunately, with a good quarterback and offensive line, I was able to maintain the lead in receptions for the state and was a first team selection to the Class 5A all-state team, an honor given to the top two receivers in the state of Texas.

The following January, I had another opportunity to showcase my skills when I was selected to the Coca-Cola High School All-Star game. This all-star game had the potential to give me the extra boost I needed before signing day and garner more interest from colleges and universities. I had a solid game, scoring the game-tying touchdown with a minute left in the fourth quarter. All-star games do not have overtime for the safety of the players, so the East tied the West 14-14.

By the time high school football was over for me, I had three official visits set up to Texas Tech, the University of North Texas and Illinois State University, in that order. I only wanted to play for Texas Tech, but my family made sure I took all of my visits in case they did not offer me a scholarship.

The Texas Tech visit was an absolute dream — all until the day I sat in former head coach Mike Leach's office and heard the exact opposite of what I was hoping to hear. He told me they were going to wait on a few other players they were recruiting; instead of giving me the scholarship I wanted, they offered a preferred walk-on spot. Or in other words, I'd be playing for free. I would be invited to training camp in the hopes that I would earn a spot on the roster, all while paying my way through school. No scholarship. While my parents thought the visit was encouraging, I did not share their sentiments at all. Texas Tech was where I wanted to go, and I had the desire, drive and production numbers that warranted a scholarship. I was floored by their reluctance to offer it to me.

My next visit was to the University of North Texas. The recruiters at North Texas were smart: they knew that I had been at Texas Tech the week prior and that I had been given a walk-on offer. In knowing that, they purposely placed me with a host player who had turned down a walk-on offer from Texas Tech and gone to North Texas instead. These guys were smart and knew exactly what they were doing. The visit went great, up until the last day. Former head coach Darrel Dickey did not offer me a scholarship, instead he said he wanted to wait and see about other players they were recruiting at the time. I felt like I was having déjà-vu from my visit to Texas Tech. I was so frustrated. Why was this happening again?

I was two visits down, with one to go. Much to my dismay, I still had no scholarship offers on the table. The one glimmer of hope I had left was my upcoming visit to Illinois State. We were really cutting things close. Once returning home from my last visit, I would have one week left before signing day. I just couldn't wrap my head around this one simple fact: how was it possible for the state receptions leader to have no college scholarship offers?

Having been disappointed by two other schools, I was a little wary as I began my visit at Illinois State. But I shouldn't have been, because the experience at Illinois State went really well. I enjoyed my visit, liked what I saw of the program and the school, and the best part of it all: I was offered my very first scholarship! It came with strings attached though. I was given a 24-hour deadline to respond. Needless to say, this was a big deal at my house. I had one scholarship offer, and one preferred walk-on offer on the table. At this point, North Texas was out of the picture completely. After a heated discussion with my family, we agreed that I would walk-on to Texas Tech and turn down a full scholarship to Illinois State. I wanted to show Texas Tech that I could play at the division one level and earn the scholarship I deserved.

With total clarity about my decision, I went in the next day feeling like I was on top of the world. Never in a million years did I see what was coming next. Before I even had the chance to turn down Illinois State's offer, North Texas called and offered me a full scholarship. I couldn't believe it. Now I had two full scholarship offers and needed to re-think my decision about walking on to Texas Tech. After a much easier discussion with my family, I couldn't turn down a full scholarship to a University in my backyard. I gave Texas Tech one more chance to see if they would match North Texas' scholarship offer, but they declined. That was it. My decision was made and I became a Mean Green Eagle! CAWWW!

CHAPTER 8

THE WEIGHT OF IT ALL

*"I am not a product of my circumstances.
I am a product of my decisions."*

– Stephen Covey

I REPORTED TO the University of North Texas at the rather underwhelming weight of 175 pounds. Nonetheless, I was ready to excel at my new division one football program! That is, until the harsh reality of my smaller size set in. I needed to put on muscle quickly in order to protect my small frame from being crushed by my giant opponents who were grown men. I remember stepping into the gym and feeling a bit intimidated seeing all the weights and machines that make up a college weight room. I knew instantly that I was going to be putting in a lot of hard work in that weight room over the next four years, and that I better get used to it very quickly. Even though I was small in stature, I really enjoyed working out, and I was looking forward to doing whatever it would take to put on muscle and become a better football player.

Thankfully, as freshmen, we had an orientation meeting in the weight room where our head strength coach and his assistants demonstrated proper technique and how to use each machine. I had already developed a pretty good understanding of how the machines worked, but this meeting proved to me just how much they were invested in making sure we had the necessary strength to play division one football. As our first day orientation came to a close, our head strength coach laid out a schedule for freshman times in the weight room. As he was talking, I was pondering whether I wanted to lift in the morning, before practice, or maybe even a night session, depending on how intense and long practice was. That was, until I realized I didn't have any options. Freshman will lift on Monday, Wednesday and Friday at 6:00 AM. Period. I remember hearing that and the first thought that crossed my mind was whether we were going to have to do that all year. And sure enough we were! When you have to get up at 5:30 AM, grab a quick snack and head to the weight room, it really sets the tone for your freshman year.

I was both excited and tired on day one. I realized instantly that my morning routine was going to be very intense. Coach sat us down and began to put us in groups of three. I could see the trend developing as to how he was forming the groups. The quarterbacks were together, the linemen were together, and the running backs were together, so naturally I was waiting for him to put the wide receivers together. Being the competitive guy that I am, I begin to check out the other wide receivers I assumed I would be paired with; I looked around the weight room and made some mental notes as to which lifts I thought I would be strongest at. And then it happened. Coach put me with two linebackers!

Now if you don't know anything about football, that's okay. Let me tell you about linebackers — they weigh 225 pounds. Now let me tell you about me — I weighed 175 pounds. I'll do the math for you. That's a 50-pound difference! I was utterly perplexed as to why my coach put me with the wrong guys for my weightlifting group. There I was, 18 years old, a young man stepping out on my own in college, and suddenly put in a group with two guys who were clearly stronger than I was in every single lifting category. So much for summing up my competition! Talk about being embarrassed — I was *mortified* every Monday, Wednesday and Friday because of the massive difference in our stature and how much stronger these guys were than me. I distinctly remember every time it was my turn to lift, they would ask me how much weight they needed to take off for me. They never said it rudely, they were just stating the facts. They would say: "What would be a good weight for you to lift, since this weight is clearly too heavy for you?"

I was mulling over a couple of different ways that I could approach my coach and get an explanation as to why in the world he would put me in a position that seemed like it was setting me up for failure. My inner monologue went something like this: *maybe he forgot I play wide receiver. Surely it isn't my size, as I look like a wide receiver? Wait, no, that's being generous. I really look more like a kicker. And if that's his rationale, why am I not with the kickers' weight lifting group?*

Regardless, I had to figure it out. So, I thought more about how I could approach my coach and ask in a way that wouldn't come off as stubborn, rude or as questioning his judgment on the group pairs. But as I was considering all of this, another possibility came to mind. What if my coach knew something that I didn't know? What if he had put me in this group on purpose, to challenge me, to push me, to encourage me to take a risk, even though it was very uncomfortable at that stage in my development? I didn't like it, but I accepted that my coach might have had a reason for what he did. Maybe it was fear of talking to my coach, or maybe it was an understanding that to play in the pro world one day, I needed to be able to overcome adversity. Either way, I decided I'd hold off on talking to my coach.

Instead, I went back and continued to hold my own with guys who were clearly bigger than I was. But let me be honest with you — I got tired of taking off the weight. I got tired of being the weak guy in the group. Over my first semester of lifting at 6:00 AM, three times a week, with two guys who were bigger and stronger than me, I could start to see myself getting stronger. It was amazing. As the weeks passed, I didn't have to take off as much weight, and soon I began to see improvements in every single one of my lifts.

Each time I'd walk into the weight room, I'd catch a glimpse of the record board. It was always there in the corner of my eye. I was eyeing that thing down — or maybe the record board was eyeing me. Either way, it felt like a challenge, and I knew that one day I wanted to see my name, under my position, on that record board. I knew I had a lot of work to do if I was going to make that a reality. As the end of my freshman year approached, it was time to test myself. I went for the power clean record for the wide receiver position, which was, at the time, set at 314 pounds. I tried multiple times, but missed again and again. On one attempt I fell to my knees trying to catch the weight and still missed it. I thought coach might have been embarrassed by how many times I went after that weight and failed, but he came up to me afterwards and let me know how proud he was of me for my efforts and desire to attempt that record. Especially since he saw how much I had grown mentally and physically over the course of my freshman year.

Although I was disappointed that I missed the record board, hearing that encouragement from my coach, from a leader in my life, reinforced all my efforts and gave me the drive to keep going and press onwards towards my goal. I didn't realize at the time how powerful his words were in my life. Can you imagine how I would have felt if my coach came over and chastised me for going after that record? If he would have belittled me in front of my teammates and friends for how stupid I was for trying to make that much of a leap in weight, especially after my performance all year as the weak one in the group? Or what if he had done something just as bad — what if he hadn't said anything at all? What if he remained quiet and carried on with business as usual? I believe those actions would have resulted in me feeling just as badly and just as discouraged as if he came over and belittled me. Sometimes saying nothing is just as bad as saying something harsh.

How many times in our lives can we look back on a situation in which we risked our reputation, or career, or efforts, all for a result that we didn't get? Did you receive encouragement from the leaders in your life for the attempt, or were you discouraged for your efforts? I truly believe the feedback you receive from the leaders in your life plays such a crucial role at that moment of failure.

It's imperative to have a leader who picks you up, reinforces your beliefs and attitude and commends your efforts; you need someone who sets in motion a positive path for you to continue to take risks, climb new heights and expand your horizons. A leader who does the opposite — who reacts negatively or does nothing and is passive towards your attempts at success — sets in motion a path of descent. That negative or passive reaction doesn't encourage thinking outside the box or taking calculated risks, but rather, the opposite. That particular path can lead to passivity and complacency, which is a death trap at the end of the road.

So, I want to challenge you. If you are in a leadership position, I want to challenge you to engage and support those in your inner circle, especially during times of risk and times of failure. Maybe it's an employee, or a child, or your neighbor who needs an extra boost of confidence as he or she explores a path that is unfamiliar and a bit risky. I challenge you to be someone that person can trust and lean on, as you just may be the kick start needed to get that person on a positive path to accomplishing something great.

I will never forget the encouragement that I received that day from my coach. Although I failed, his response set in motion attitudes and actions to break through barriers down the road that might have kept me from achieving my goals. In fact, by the time I left the University of North Texas, I was fortunate enough to have set the power clean record, the bench press record and the incline press record. I set the bench press record during the summer between my junior and senior year in college, and I invited my dad to come and watch as I made my attempt. I thought that it seemed like some extra manly stuff to invite my dad to be part of. So there we all were in the weight room; with so much weight, the bar was bending. My dad was so excited to see his son be there under that kind of weight and then complete the lift successfully. It was pretty special having him there for that moment and to hear his words of encouragement.

Now I'm going to press the fast-forward button to 10 years later, during Olympic qualifications, where I became the first athlete at the Olympic Training Center in Lake Placid, New York to power clean over 400 pounds. It was a huge milestone in my career, and it couldn't have come at a better time, as I was trying to make the U.S. Olympic Team. I remember preparing my mind to lift that weight and set the new record. I was overwhelmed with thankfulness and gratitude for the support and encouragement I had in my life then, and throughout my entire journey. That mindset reinforced the confidence I needed in order to crush the weight that was sitting in front of me. The 400 pounds felt heavy, but at the same time, it also felt light, as weird as that might sound. I was focused,

I was ready and I was in what athletes call "The Zone." I wasn't just lifting this weight for myself; I was going to break this record for everyone who believed in me along my path of ups and downs, failures and successes, and were always there to keep me moving in the right direction!

When I finally lifted the weight, the joy I felt was impossible to describe. I could hear the cheers and excitement that filled the Olympic Training Center weight room. My adrenaline was out the roof, and I was flooded with so many emotions and sheer excitement. I was thankful for the moments, both good and bad, that lead to that moment. As I reflect on that milestone, there is no doubt in my mind that the words of motivation during times of failure pushed me through and allowed me to accomplish that and so many other big feats. So let me ask you, how do you respond to failure? How do you respond to success? Better yet, are you able to encourage, listen and motivate those in your life who are struggling right now?

We don't have to be perfect, but we do have to be present. My hope is that during times of success and times of failure that we can create enough margin to realize we need other people in our life that can provide guidance and encouragement during different seasons of our life.

CHAPTER 9

RIDING THE BENCH

"What I know for sure is that what you give comes back to you."

– Oprah Winfrey

THE WEIGHT ROOM during my freshman year was tough, but what was even tougher was riding the bench. Being an undersized wide receiver, I realized stepping on a college campus I had room to grow — both physically and mentally — so I was a prime candidate to be what's called "redshirted." To redshirt means that you are allowed to lift, practice and travel with the team, but you can't play. Redshirting is very common for incoming freshman as a way to help ease their transition from high school to college. Looking back on it now, redshirting was the best thing that could have happened to me that year. It gave me a chance to learn and study the playbook, develop my body for college football and help transition to college schoolwork and the demands of being a full-time student-athlete. What I didn't anticipate was the feeling of being left out or lonely. When you redshirt, it doesn't feel like you are truly a part of the team. Sure I was at practice every day and doing my very best to give the starters my full effort in order to prepare them for the upcoming games. But when it came to team activities, I just felt like the redshirts were outcasts, since there was no chance of us playing the entire season.

I remember halfway through my redshirt season I was on a practice team, and I would go full speed on every play. It didn't matter if it was a pass play or a run play, you could count on me going full speed. I did this for two reasons: I wanted our team to win, so the only way I could contribute during my redshirt year was to prepare the defense the best I could. Secondly, I knew that one day I wanted to play in the NFL, and if that dream was going to come to pass, it was imperative that I do everything to prepare my body and mind for the NFL level.

However, not everyone saw it the same way. I came to find out that the starters on defense and the upperclassmen did not like when freshman went full speed and gave maximum effort on every play. This is because sometimes the freshmen would win, and that didn't look good for the others. In particular, it didn't look very good the next day when they would be reviewing the film with coach, and he would say: "Hey, what happened here? Why did you let a freshman beat you on this play?" I would receive some nasty comments asking why I had tried so hard. Sometimes I would take a cheap shot from an upperclassman in practice as he made an effort to show me how things needed to be done — or at least to slow me down. Unfortunately for them, it only added fuel to my fire and I continued to practice with guns blazing regardless of the poor feedback I was receiving from the upperclassmen, as I knew what my ultimate goal was.

There's one play I remember distinctly from October of my redshirt freshman year. We were working around the goal line, giving the defense potential looks and plays they might see as our opponent approached the scoring position. I ran a three-step slant route and caught the football for a quick touchdown. Since I scored, the defensive coordinator was not pleased with the guy covering me, so he had us run the exact same play to show the defender how to properly position himself versus a potential slant route at the goal line. As a practice team member, we do exactly as the coach tells us, even if that means running the exact same play again. Keep in mind that because we are running the exact same play again, the defense clearly knows what to expect. Although we ran the same play, I sincerely thought our practice team quarterback would look for a different option as to where to throw the football, since the guy guarding me was now standing in the passing lane between the end zone and me. Instead, the quarterback zipped the ball back into the slant window, which was now occupied by the defender. Naturally, I tried to knock the ball down to keep it from being intercepted. In doing so, my finger got stuck, and the ball hit the top of my pinky and pushed it down and back into my hand, breaking and dislocating the knuckle.

As I looked down at my hand, I knew immediately that something was wrong. My pinky knuckle was facing the wrong direction. I showed my coach what had happened. I pointed at my hand and its newly deformed shape and then calmly walked over to the trainer to let him know that I had a small problem with one of my fingers. I left for the hospital to get an x-ray to see exactly what the damage was. I was hoping it was just dislocated and that a simple "pop-back-in-place" would be the course of treatment. To my dismay, it turned out the injury was more serious than that and required surgery. A day or so later I had my pinky secured and put back in place. This was the first of what would eventually be four surgeries, all on different body parts, that I would have to have throughout my football career.

As I reflect back on that time as an undersized freshman wide receiver, I remember thinking that I could go through the motions and let the starters on defense practice in cruise control, but what good would that do me in the long run? I remember the feeling of being embarrassed because I practiced full speed every day and every play, yet some of the guys in leadership positions, A.K.A. the starters on defense, would make fun of me for trying too hard in practice. Have you felt that before, where it seemed like people were making fun of you, or ignoring you because of your efforts to do things the right way? Maybe it's someone in a leadership position in your life, or someone in a group or team at your office that tries to cap your efforts because, "it's just not how things are done at this level."

Can I just encourage you to continue to give your best effort every day, every hour and every moment, regardless of the naysayers out there? As I continued to practice full speed, learn, and give maximum effort, I started to notice a couple of things. I started to notice the gap between talent began to shrink. What I mean by that is, I was exerting maximum effort on every single play, while at the same time, some of the upperclassmen continued lazily going through the motions. In other words, I got better, while they stayed the same. I began to improve my technique, my consistency and my ability to react and process information faster every single day. The upperclassmen that chose to take it easy did not improve every day. In fact, in some cases, their choice of going through the motions set in motion negative habits. Soon enough, their starting position on the team was replaced by an underclassman who not only closed the gap in talent, but also surpassed it, due to their lack of willingness to participate at full speed on a consistent basis.

As you read this, I would imagine that you would have the common sense response of also deciding to go full speed, give maximum effort and continuing to learn and grow every day. I think it is safe to say that with the above example, we would all choose to be the underclassman closing the gap and catching the upperclassman who displayed laziness and unwillingness to make himself and the team better. But what does that look like in real life? What does that look like for you, if you're not a football player? How can we be the former and not the latter at our home, at our school, at our place of employment and in our community? The first step is understanding that you have a choice. That it doesn't matter your income level, social status, what car you drive, where you live or where you vacation. Each day you have a choice, and that choice is to go through the motions or give full effort. On paper, we know the right answer, but in real life with the pressure of outside influences and potentially being labeled "not cool," it can make it very difficult to display maximum effort in everything we do.

CHAPTER 10

BECOMING A STARTER

"If you always put limits on everything you do, physical or anything else, it will spread into your work and into your life. There are no limits. There are only plateaus, and you must not stay there, you must go beyond them."

– Bruce Lee

I HAD THE first year of college classes, football practices and scheduling under my belt. I jumped up from 175 pounds, to 181 pounds, to 195 pounds in 12 months. My body looked more like a division one football player and less like a prepubescent teenager. I was ready to go after my dream and earn a starting spot on the roster. I was competing against a senior whose brother was already playing in the NFL. He had strong genes and looked the part of the dominant college wide receiver. Going into the first game, I was second string behind the senior wide receiver. We opened the season versus the Oklahoma Sooners. If you haven't been to Norman, Oklahoma, let me tell you something — the stadium is rocking! It was raining and just a nasty day, but it was my first football game at a big-time division one program and I wanted to soak in all the emotions of being on the big stage. The senior receiver who started the game had two penalties for not lining up correctly. If you're not familiar with football, that's a rookie mistake. Coach had me sub in for him early on, and I didn't look back. I finished the night in Norman with three catches for 37 yards, which started my streak of having a reception every game for 47 consecutive games. It turns out, that would be the third-longest streak in the nation at the time I played my last college football game four years later.

We lost that game to OU and, as fate would have it, OU went on to win the national championship that year. But what it did for me was set in motion a drive to get better and improve in every aspect of my game. That game, there were a couple plays where I felt more than a little embarrassed. One of them involved Derrick Strait, a defender on Oklahoma's secondary, an Associated Press All-American and a candidate for the Jim Thorpe award. The Jim Thorpe award is given to the best defensive back in the nation. He ended up winning that award at the end of the year. I found out first hand during that game exactly why he deserved to be coined the top defensive back in all of college football.

We had just finished third down and came up short, so it was time to punt. We ran a quick punt spread to try and catch the defense off guard. I was lined up versus OU's top defensive back, and now that we were punting, my objective changed from being the wide receiver to being a punt cover player that needed to sprint 40 yards down the field and tackle their returner. The only person in my way was this All-American defensive back.

When we snapped the ball, I didn't even know what hit me. I remember not being able to even get off the line of scrimmage. He got into my shoulder pads before I even had a chance to move, and I couldn't go anywhere. I tried to club his arms to get him off me, but he didn't budge. It was like a freight train hit me. He locked in even tighter, and his strength overpowered mine. He moved me in a direction I did not want to go. By the time the play was over, I had made no progress down the field and had failed in my duty as the punt cover guy. I ended up on the ground with my helmet shoved up my nose and a confused look on my face, trying to figure out what in the world had just happened. He had turned me around and brought me down to the ground.

Although that was only one play, it was a play that I vividly remember. On the bus ride home from Oklahoma, I vowed that I would never let that happen again. This guy was clearly stronger than me, and he displayed his power in such a way that I couldn't do a dang thing. I did not like that feeling at all. Not only did I not like it, I was also downright embarrassed and hoped Coach wouldn't show that play to the entire team the next day during film review.

I couldn't get that particular play out of my mind. Even though I had my first college reception that night (three to be exact), which was a milestone moment, it was the punt play where I got owned that replayed in my mind. I was dreading film review with my teammates. I could already picture the gasps when coach played the film in slow motion during my on-the-field assault. Surely, I would lose my newly appointed starting position because of that particular play.

Have you ever thought about that one situation, one action or one moment that didn't go the way you anticipated? It takes over your entire thought process, and you wish you could have a do-over with an entirely different outcome. If this is you, don't worry — you're not alone, we all do this. It's like a downward spiral effect that can be extremely exhausting and time-consuming. I could not get that one particular play out of my mind.

The next day, we watched the film together as a team. I began to feel a sense of dread as we got closer to the punt play. It was like the part in a scary movie where you know what's about to happen and you want to cover your eyes. Finally, it was time to review the play and coach focused on the fundamental breakdown in our coverage as a unit, and not the mistakes made by any one particular player (thankfully). I could hear a little bit of bickering in the back of the room, and while I was pretty certain they were discussing my beat down, I didn't have 100% confirmation. I liked to think they were discussing what was on the cafeteria menu for the evening, or perhaps an upcoming test, or how hot the Texas heat was for practice.

Regardless, coach moved on to the next play, and it was done. The outcome I had come to in my mind, which was the worst-case, most embarrassing scenario, never came to fruition. That meeting proved to be a pivotal point of growth for me, not only as an athlete, but also as a person. The sum of the team is greater than one person, I realized. In my mind, it was absolutely mortifying. But our coach — the leader in the room — looked at the big picture and addressed the fundamental issue of an entire team's communication breaking down, as opposed to singling out one person and shifting the blame to them.

As we journey through life and the teams we are on at home, at work and in the community, let us concern ourselves with the entire vision of the team and how the team is operating and functioning as a whole. Too many times we focus on our own lack of production, or on our inability to measure up. When you are on a team — and we all are on a team in some form or fashion — we can lean into each other and work together towards the outcome we are looking to achieve. It truly is for the best.

CHAPTER 11

BACK TO EMBARRASSMENT

*"If it's important to you, you will find a way.
If not, you'll find an excuse."*

– Ryan Blair

MY COLLEGE FOOTBALL career got off to a great start. It turned out redshirting was the best thing for me. It gave me a chance to develop physically and mentally for division one football. After the first game at Oklahoma, I became a starter and never looked back. I was fortunate enough to earn all-conference honors my first year, which gave me an enormous amount of confidence heading into the off-season. But I knew that I needed to continue to improve if I wanted to make it to the NFL someday.

Now let's rewind a little bit. If you remember what I told you about my high school career, you'll remember that one of my coaches walked me through the importance of running track and how it related to football early on — and that I bought in to his vision. I could see firsthand that learning to run with proper technique in track made me a better wide receiver. Putting those pieces together, it made logical sense for me to walk-on to the UNT track and field team. I ran track in high school and was decent, but I knew this was going to be a whole new ball game at the collegiate level.

The first step was getting permission from my head football coach to allow me to compete in track. I was on full scholarship, so my future track career would lean solely on the willingness of my football coach to allow this side venture. It was the first hurdle I had to get over, no pun intended.

I remember approaching his office and getting ready to knock on the door when I noticed he had a couple of other coaches in with him reviewing game tapes. I was really nervous and got straight to business. "Hey, Coach," I said. "Can I run track this spring?" He stared at me with this perplexed look on his face, and paused for what felt like forever. He finally broke the awkward silence and asked how my grades were. I told him they were good, but he still looked to one of the other coaches in the room that was in charge of academic monitoring of all the football players for confirmation. The coach in charge of grades nodded slightly, supporting my claim and verifying my statement was accurate. After clearing the first stage of permission with good academic standing, I then fielded questions on my rationale for wanting to run track.

I explained: "I need to get faster." To which my coach said, "Are you trying to get out of off-season practice with the team?" I was caught completely off guard by his response, as that notion had really never crossed my mind. However, it did bring the realization that my off-season days would now turn into two-a-day practices. I definitely missed that when I was analyzing everything and thought running track was a good idea. My football coach wanted to make sure that I didn't miss any practices and closed the proverbial door to any inkling that I was trying to get out of football practice by running track. For the next two spring semesters, I would step into the weight room at 6:00 AM for my football workout, head to class from 8:00 AM - 1:00 PM, grab a bite to eat and then head to the track at 3:00 PM for track practice. By 5:30 PM, I was exhausted.

While my football coaches were clearly testing my motives to see if I would break, I had a track and field coach that showed an unbelievable amount of grace towards my efforts of competing in two collegiate sports at the division one level. He would routinely ask me about my football workout in the morning, what type of volume we did and how my body felt six hours later. He would take my honest feedback and help customize my workout in track practice to get the efforts he desired without my body falling apart from overtraining and sheer fatigue.

Track is a different story than football. In football, if you are not playing, you can put your helmet on, hide your number on the sideline with 85 other teammates and no one knows where you are in the shuffle of people that make up the sideline. In other words, no one knows if you're not playing. Now in track and field, it is a whole different ball game. There are no helmets, no sidelines — just you, in a speed suit, in a lane all by yourself. If you are taking last place, everyone knows who is coming in last place. My first two years running college track were humbling, to say the least. I took last place in the 100- and 200-meter dash. The worst part about coming in last place would be on the following Monday when our coach would display the meet results for everyone to see in the locker room. I dreaded heading to practice on Mondays because I knew everyone would see how poorly I had performed over the weekend. Walking into the locker room and seeing my name at the bottom of the list in the 100- and 200-meter dash was humiliating. I don't know if I was more embarrassed about my performance, or the fact that my friends saw how badly I had done.

At that point, I had a couple of options. I could go to my track coach, the leader in my life and say, "Hey coach, track has been fun (not really), but you know I am a football player and my scholarship is in football so I think I should probably go back to where I feel the most comfortable." The more I would play this scenario of returning to football out in my head, the more sense it made. I was tired of taking a four to five-hour bus ride only to take last place. And I would think to myself, it's off-season time and my buddies are at the lake enjoying their time off while I'm over here grinding on overtime… and for what? I'm really not that good at track and field; I'm probably just taking up space. Surely there is someone else who could take my spot and put my speed suit to better use. This was my internal monologue, and I would play it over and over like it was on repeat in my head.

This thought process was easy. It was what came naturally. I could sit there and feed these thoughts and emotions. On the other hand, I knew there was also a different approach; a more challenging approach. The other approach was a bit tougher, but in the end, it was exactly what I needed. This scenario was to listen to my coach, one of the leaders in my life, with an understanding that he might know something that I didn't know just yet. His experience over the course of several decades as a college track coach could provide me with wisdom in my young career.

Now let me be honest with you, the second option was not the most attractive, mainly because I kept taking last place in our track meets, which was utterly embarrassing. That being said, my end goal was to one day play in the NFL, and in order for that dream to come true, I knew I had to get faster. There was simply no other way around that, especially since I played wide receiver, which required a ton of speed.

Weighing all my options, I chose option two. I was going to stick it out and trust in the leadership of my coach. I also got tired of taking last place. I started small. I knew with enough effort, I could beat at least one person. And I steadily began to get faster and faster. I started to pick one competitor off after another. I remember the first time I cracked into the top 10 for the 100-meter dash. We were running at the TCU relays, and I was in a lane next to one of Texas Tech's fastest sprinters. I remember watching him in high school, and thinking, this guy could move! When I saw the heat line up and realized we would be next to each other in the starting blocks, I knew if I could stay close to him, I would run fast.

My goal was to get out of the blocks and trail just behind him in his hip pocket throughout the entire race. At the end, I would make my move to see if I could pass him and win the heat. I got out of the blocks fast and could see out of my peripheral vision that he was slightly ahead. I was thrilled at being so close to him as we passed the 50-meter mark. I tried to kick it into overdrive to see if I could pass him on the remainder of the race, but I just didn't have enough gas in the tank to make the move. He beat me, but only by a small margin. I was so pumped and couldn't wait to see the results. I knew my time would be fast since I had hung by him the whole race.

Have you experienced that feeling? Have you felt a bit overwhelmed because someone in your life is uber-talented? Have you had the recurring thought that you don't measure up, or that you don't have what it takes to succeed? Running track was very humbling for me, because at face value I was not very good at it. However, I knew that in order to accomplish my long-term goal of one day becoming a professional football player, running track was necessary to develop the tools that I needed for that bigger dream to come to fruition. For that to happen, there had to be a shift in my mindset; an understanding that all things work together, even in areas where we might struggle or not perform at a high level.

As I crossed the finish line in second place, knowing that my time was going to be one of my best, I waited in anticipation to see what the scoreboard was going to read to all in attendance. On that day, I ran the fastest 100-meter dash time of my career at 10.62 seconds. Now, 10.6 isn't an elite time, but it certainly isn't a time for a slouch either. Running a 10.6 was important for my growth as a person because it demonstrated in real time that hard work does pay off. When I got recruited out of high school (or lack thereof), my biggest knock was my height and speed. Many recruiters felt that I didn't have the top end speed it took to play at the next level. Although I didn't want to agree with their evaluation of me, they did have a point, as I just wasn't all that fast. Maybe it was a chip on my shoulder from hearing those negative reviews about my speed, or maybe it was an unbelievable desire to one day play in the NFL, but either way, I got faster. By the time I left the University of North Texas, I had earned a spot as the anchor leg on our 4x100 sprint relay and was fortunate enough to anchor our sprint relay to a conference championship and a trip to the NCAA Regional Track & Field Meet. We ran the third fastest time in school history at 39.92; to see my name on the track and field record board solidified that hard work does pay off.

I ran all four years at the University of North Texas, and when the NFL scouts came for our pro day, I ran the fastest 40-yard dash time of all the receivers at 4.42 seconds. Each year, the NFL scouts would come to UNT to test all the football players. I had the date circled and marked on my calendar, as I knew it was a chance to set the record for receivers. When I ran that time, a sense of joy and happiness flowed through my veins. I couldn't help but think of my high school days and the long hours spent on the track in college to prepare me for this moment.

But the day didn't start off quite so well. As I woke up that morning for testing, the strangest thing happened: I couldn't open my eye. I ran to the bathroom to see why in the world my eye wouldn't open. It was crusted over, and as I rubbed it all away, I could see my eye was red. It turns out that I had pink eye and needed to immediately see the doctor for help — and hopefully a quick remedy. He prescribed medicine and an eye ointment for me, but all I kept thinking was *not today, please not today!* Out of all the days this could've happened, it had to happen on the day the NFL scouts were coming to test? I asked the doctor if I would be ok to do my testing and he said I would, as long as I protected my eye. Leaving the doctor's office a few hours before the biggest athletic test of my life, I was relieved that I could compete, but also mentally drained at the astonishment of why this was happening on this particular day. Out of all the days, why today? Why? If I didn't think it would be overly dramatic, I would've knelt down on my knees with hands folded, looked up towards the sky and yelled, "Why me, why me?" I didn't kneel down, but I did keep repeating that question in my mind over and over on the way back to my apartment. The stress of it was exhausting, and by the time I got there, all I wanted to do was lie down before I had to report to the field house.

As I lay in my apartment, trying to keep my mind off my eye and the devastating timing of pink eye, I remember having this calm feeling rush over me. I had a feeling of stillness and a sense of relief that I was prepared for this moment. Although the situation was difficult and I would have preferred for that not to happen that day, I wasn't going to let it impact my production. My big day had arrived: I had prepared, I had put in the work and I was ready to showcase everything I had been working for — regardless of the weather, my mood or even pink eye. You see, I was ready for my moment, and I was not going to let anything keep me from the opportunity to capitalize on my moment.

I'm sure I looked goofy running the 40-yard dash in sunglasses to protect my eye, but to see my time and watch the scouts take a second look at their timers to confirm that I just ran the fastest 40-yard dash time on the team was an unbelievable moment. A 4.42 second 40-yard dash time, the fastest of my career, couldn't have come at a better time. What is even crazier is that I had a track meet that evening, so I had to quickly gather my belongings, high-five my coaches and teammates and head back to my apartment to get off my legs and rest for the track meet that evening.

I remember lying in bed absolutely thrilled at how well the testing had gone in front of my potential future employer. I had a chance to pause and thank God for providing for me in a time of need, during a time of uncertainty, when I couldn't get my mind off my situation — the poor timing of the pink eye. He delivered because His plan is perfect, all the time. That evening we won the 4x100m relay and qualified for the NCAA regional meet by running a season-best time of 39.99. That was our first time as a team to run the relay in less than 40 seconds. It was a perfect ending to a not-so-perfect day.

Running track was one of the best decisions I made during my college career. Although I did not know it at the time, running track in college would prepare me for my future path to the Olympics in the sport of bobsled. The similarities between track and bobsled run parallel in a lot of aspects. In track, you have to learn how to warm up properly and keep your body warm between events. Some track meets literally last all day long, so there is a process each track athlete must know when preparing for warm-ups and cool downs. Bobsled can operate similarly in that regard. Some bobsled races literally take hours with track delays. In each race, there is unfortunately at least one crash, which slows things down. Being a mountain sport, most of the time it's snowing at the bobsled track, which also slows down the pace between each sled and competition heat. I can remember bobsled races where two hours would pass between each push. I think you get the picture. There was a lot of waiting in both sports, and in situations like this, track preparation in college would become very handy in preparing for bobsled races.

Athletically speaking, running track at the division one level was one of the biggest embarrassments of my career. I never came close to the accolades and accomplishments I received in football. Track was a real struggle for me, but it turned out to be a fertile ground of preparation for my future. As I look back on my track career, there are a couple takeaways. For starters, I am glad that I didn't quit. Had I quit track just because I wasn't good at it, I would have never developed into the athlete I needed to be in order to qualify for an Olympic team, and I would have stunted my mental growth. Secondly, because I wasn't naturally talented in track, I learned that I had to give maximum effort during track practice and meets instead of just coasting along and going through the motions. Showing up is half the battle, but once you arrive, it is crucial that you give maximum effort to reap your desired reward. I think some people miss that. In this day and age, where social media connects us all, I think we as a society tend to forget that in order to accomplish your goals, you will need to apply full effort, every single day, to reach your dream. In hindsight, consistency and discipline are two of the most important lessons I learned through athletics.

Is there something in your life that you're not so good at, or struggle with but know it will help you in the long run? The frustration is present because it's challenging, and it may be difficult to see the reward at the end because you're being blinded by the toughness. But here's what I want you to know: there is always a reward at the end. You just have to keep going. You have to keep pushing through the pain. The reward may not come in the form you think it will. Mine certainly didn't. It came by way of the Olympic bobsled team, and nobody could have predicted that. Your reward may also come at a later point in time than what you were expecting, but if you work hard enough, it will always come! The reward will be there if you don't give up and continue to put in the full effort to complete the task at hand. Spend some time thinking about an area of your life that meets the requirements for this chapter. I want you to know that you are on the right path!

CHAPTER 12

BROKEN RECORDS, BROKEN BONES

"If you have a beautiful story, it has to have conflict. If you don't have conflict, it can't be a good story."

– Donald Miller

PLAYING FOUR YEARS of college football and running four years of college track put me in an excellent position to make my dream of becoming a professional athlete come true. I could feel the anticipation about turning pro at the beginning of my senior year of college, and I was ready to capitalize on it. I was excited to be on the verge of accomplishing a lifelong dream but, at the same time, knew there was still plenty of work to be done.

Two-a-days in Texas are hot! The term refers to a period in which football teams practice once in the morning and again in the afternoon. The summer heat and multiple practices really weed out the pretenders from the contenders as everyone prepares for a strong season. Prior to my junior football season, our team won three conference championships and played in three NCAA bowl games. Needless to say, it was an exciting time. But the previous year had been a down year as we only won two games and lost nine. Everyone on the team had a sour taste in their mouths from that year, and we were ready to get back on track as a mid-major powerhouse. I was chosen to be a team captain for the second year in a row. It was an honor and something that I never took for granted — the trust the others put in me to be one of the captains and lead the direction of our team.

I was also eyeing a few personal records that year. I remember first stepping on campus as an undersized freshman football player and seeing all the receiving records listed at the back of the football program. Throughout my college career I had dreamed of leaving as the school's all-time leading receiver; now I was within striking distance of making that dream a reality. Also, as it turned out, I was sitting third in the nation for most consecutive games with a reception and was nominated to the pre-season Biletnikoff Watch List. The Biletnikoff award is given each year to the best wide receiver in college football. I was ecstatic for my senior season.

It was about two weeks before our first game, and we were wrapping up our two-day schedule. We were getting tired of tackling each other and ready to play our first opponent. We would open the season against the Texas Longhorns in Austin, Texas at Darrell K. Royal Stadium. This was a huge opponent for us and a pretty special place to play football as the stadium held roughly 90,000 people at the time. That's a lot of people watching football, screaming their heads off for the home team. The atmosphere as an away team in a stadium that loud and that packed is pretty hostile. I have never heard that many people "boo" in cadence. Ever.

As practice began to wrap up, we were finishing a morning session of 7-on-7. The 7-on-7 is a drill where the quarterback and receivers run routes versus the defensive backs. It is all passing plays. There are no running plays during 7-on-7. Sometimes it can be unfair for the wide receivers because the defense already knows it's going to be a pass, which makes my job as a wide receiver even tougher.

I lined up in the slot position and ran a seam route — a straight line down the field. That is, run as fast as possible. For whatever reason, I was left open, and the quarterback threw a perfect pass. But the play had ended with the ball still in the air and, as I jogged back to the huddle, I got slugged in the back. My neck whiplashed from the unexpected hit, and I went crashing to the ground. I was furious, and I turned to look at the culprit that had committed this violent and unforgiveable act. He was a junior college transfer with a chip on his shoulder. In a less than stellar moment, I threw the ball at him and started yelling. Testosterone levels were high, and this lead to what is known as a "football fight."

Football fights are different than real fights. First of all, both people are wearing full pads, which protect most of the body, and helmets, which protect the face and head. Secondly, a football fight is over once teammates and coaches break up the fight. And by the time the fight ends, so does the animosity between teammates. It's over, and it's just part of the game. Ask someone you know who played football and they will articulate the same concept when it comes to football fights. You fight, it gets broken up and it's over. Everyone moves on. It happens in that order, and it is very common to see during two a days when everyone is tired, exhausted and running on fumes.

The problem with this particular football fight is that I was a big dummy and hit my teammate's helmet so hard with my fist that I broke a bone. X-rays showed that I had broken the third metatarsal in my hand, which would require surgery to place two screws and wire in place to fix the broken bone. This left our training staff scrambling to devise a game plan for getting me back on football field as soon as possible.

Finding out I needed surgery ten days before the beginning of my senior season was a devastating blow. First of all, how could I be so dumb and fight my teammate — a guy that I would go to battle with shortly — and break my hand? Second of all, how could I, as the team captain, have put my teammates in this position? I had selfishly chosen to respond badly to a questionable hit during a routine football drill, and that decision was now going to cost the team. I felt utterly awful.

I was in surgery the next day, and thankfully everything went well. I came out of surgery ready for the action plan our team doctors had put together to get me back on the field. We found out that the NCAA allows you to play with a cast, but you must have a certain amount of padding around the cast, otherwise it is deemed a weapon. Shortly after surgery, we were en route to downtown Dallas to meet with a hand specialist. They wanted to fit my cast with a custom neoprene sleeve that would protect the cast and satisfy the NCAA requirements so my cast would not be seen as a weapon on the football field.

I was thrilled for a solution to get back to the game, but also a little bewildered as to how this was all going to work. The cast, along with my neoprene sleeve, covered my left middle finger, ring finger and pinky finger. These three fingers were now rendered useless to catch a football. As a wide receiver, having all ten fingers is typically a must when catching a pass. For the next couple of weeks, I would be left with only seven fingers ready for action. That was going to be a real challenge.

Our first game of the season versus the University of Texas didn't go smoothly. The Longhorns gave us a real whooping on national television, all while I was secretly trying to figure out how to make seven fingers work like ten fingers. I had four receptions that game, which kept my consecutive reception streak alive at third in the nation. But the game was still a bust.

Our next opponent was our cross-town rival Southern Methodist University (SMU). The Dallas Fort Worth metroplex is made up of three top colleges: The University of North Texas (UNT), where I attended; Texas Christian University (TCU), and SMU. When we played each other in any sport, especially football, the fan turnout was always top-notch because the travel was relatively easy for both teams. Hosting SMU at home for our season opener made the week of preparation one of high intensity. Both teams wanted bragging rights for the next year, making it a tough battle.

In typical football fashion, it was common for our offensive coordinator to script the first five-to-ten plays of the game. It gives players a chance to see certain kinds of coverage, and it gives our coaches in the press box a better idea of how the game might play out against certain plays. I found out early on that the first play of the game would be a play-action pass to me: Mr. Seven Fingers. Play-action means the quarterback fakes handing the ball off to the running back in hopes of tricking the defense into thinking that it is a running play. During the trickery, the receiver (me) is supposed to act like he is going to block and then take off like a firecracker down the field for a long pass — and hopefully a long completion.

I must have forgotten I only had seven fingers on this play as I set my defender up nicely to sell the run play, then hit the gas and ran down the field! The ball was a bit underthrown, so I had to slow down and time my jump perfectly with the SMU defender sitting in my hip pocket. The ball was out of reach for the defender, but right in my line of view. I snatched the football out of the air as the defender dove and grabbed me by the waist to take me to the ground. I guess the defender thought the impact of the ground might help jar the ball loose, but I had other plans. My seven fingers locked the ball into my rib cage as I felt the impact from the defender. We both landed on the ground together, and sure enough, the ball was in a death grip in both of my hands — even minus three fingers — and it wasn't going anywhere. I immediately heard the crowd go wild with cheers of excitement. I looked at my wide receiver coach who had a look of amazement on his face; he gave me two thumbs up as the play had been successful!

We ended up beating SMU that night 24-6, proudly earning bragging rights in the metroplex for the next year. I finished the game with ten receptions for 128 receiving yards, one of my best performances statistically as a college football player. A few of the SMU players came up to me after the game to inspect my cast and share words of both disbelief and praise that I was able to play with only seven fingers. I was pleased that we won our home opener versus our cross-town rival, and just as happy that I would be getting my cast off before our next game.

When the cast came off, it felt amazing! Finally, I could use all my fingers to catch a football the way it was designed to be caught. I felt like a brand-new man playing the next two football games as a regular human being. Just when I was getting used to being 100 percent, the injury bug struck again.

It was a mid-week practice — no pads, just helmets — and we were running routes on air. Routes on air are when the offense is doing drills without the defense. We call it "on air" because there are no defenders guarding us as we work on routes literally on air. A lot of teams do this type of drill to fine-tune existing plays and to implement new plays. We were working on a new play where I was lined up in the backfield as a running back. My responsibility on this particular play was to line up next to the quarterback in the backfield, and when the ball was snapped, to run a swing route. A swing route is a short route that stretches the defense. I start in the backfield and then run and swing to the sideline as fast as I can to out-leverage the defense.

The ball was snapped; I sprinted to the sideline and caught the ball in stride. As I put my left foot on the ground to shift my momentum up field, I felt a snap. It was a giant snap and immediately pain shot up my leg. I stopped running and looked around, as I initially thought that some-one had stepped on my ankle. But it was impossible for someone to have stepped on my ankle because we were running routes on air. Remember, there were no defenders when we ran routes on air, only the air! I looked down at my ankle and could see it start to swell around my cleat. I had my ankles taped for practice, and the swelling was even elevating the tape around my left ankle.

I hobbled over to our head trainer and filled him in on the problem. I said, "I can't run. Something happened to my ankle, and I'm not quite sure what, but I can't run." The head trainer took off my cleat and cut the tape around my ankle to investigate the problem area. Once the tape was removed, it was clear that I wouldn't be running for a while. My ankle looked like a bowling ball. All four sides puffed up and were already turn-ing black and blue. "Well, I think we've found the problem, Johnny!" the trainer said half joking until he saw the serious look on my face. "Let's get you off the field and over to the doctor. This is going to require an MRI to see what's going on."

I hobbled to the locker room in disbelief. I had just finished nursing my hand injury from the beginning of the season, and now I was facing a severe ankle injury. I thought to myself: *You've got to be kidding. How much worse can my senior season get?* Turns out, it got worse. The MRI showed that I had dislocated and torn two tendons in my ankle, which would require surgery to fix. Man, at that rate, I needed a frequent flier card for the hospital!

Unlike the surgery I had at the beginning of the season on my hand, this surgery would end my football season. The recovery demanded a mini-mum of eight weeks post-surgery with no weight on my ankle. I thought to myself, crutches for eight weeks? There was no way I could finish out the football season on a pair of crutches. I asked if there were any other options, and to my surprise, the doctor actually said yes. My ears perked up and my eyes locked in on his next statement. He said, "You will need surgery, but we can postpone surgery until the end of the season." A glimmer of hope seeped back into my heart after I heard those words. That was until I stood up and tried to walk and immediately felt the excruciating pain shoot up my leg from my ankle. I quickly grabbed the table to offset the weight I had just placed on my left ankle and said, "How can I play on a bum ankle when I can't even walk?" The doctor has an immediate response, as if he was already anticipating the litany of questions I had. "Well, we are going to numb your ankle before the game and put a soft cast on your foot to limit full motion."

The plan was to shoot my ankle up with lidocaine before the game in order to numb the area so I wouldn't feel the pain of running, jumping and cutting on my ankle. My memory went right to the movie *Varsity Blues* and the scene where the team doctor is shooting up the star player's knee so he could play. In that particular situation, that was a big no-no as that did additional damage. The look on my face must have said it all because the doctor calmly and confidently told me that the damage to my ankle was already done and that it would require surgery. There was no way around that. He then went on to explain that I wouldn't do any additional damage to the area by playing and there was no risk of long-term damage by postponing the surgery a few weeks in order to finish out the season.

My NFL dreams flashed before me as I knew this would be a major hurdle to overcome and the first thing scouts would look at is my ankle to make sure it was 100 percent healed. This put me in a tough situation. On one hand, I could have the surgery now, end my football season and begin to focus on the NFL draft. This option provided the fastest recovery timeline if the NFL was my number one priority.

The other option was to play on my broken ankle, finish the season and have surgery once the season was complete. This option would delay my preparation for the NFL draft, but it would allow me to finish out the season with my teammates. This would be the last time I would play college football with the guys I cared the most about. I guess you could say I was feeling a tad nostalgic. Also in reach were the school records for most receptions and most receiving yards in North Texas Football history. Keep in mind that I had been eyeing these records since I stepped on campus as a freshman!

I weighed my options; my decision was a no-brainer. I would postpone surgery and continue to battle on the football field with my teammates for the remainder of the year. I still had concerns about my ankle — the numbing and the limited range of motion with a soft cast. My family decided to do a little bit more due diligence and get a second and third opinion about playing on two torn ligaments and the potential for long-term damage. After the other doctors reviewed the MRI, examined my ankle and reviewed the plan of action, their outcome and diagnosis was the same as that of the team doctors. I would need surgery no matter what, and playing on the ankle to finish out the season would not cause any more damage after what had already happened.

Our team doctor instructed me that the numbing of my ankle would take place one hour before the game. Therefore, during the week of practice, I wasn't able to run or practice with the team. The pain was too excruciating. Instead, I had a separate workout, which consisted of riding a stationary bike to work my lungs and stay in sound cardiovascular shape without putting any impact on my ankle. It was not an ideal situation because I hated missing practice and being there with my teammates, but it was the only scenario that could prepare me the most for game day.

As game day approached, the first one I would play with a numb ankle, I walked into the training room eager to get on the playing field. The team doctor had the needle ready and waiting. It was a double-edged sword, or should I say, needle. I liked to see that we were all ready to go, but I also didn't like to see that large needle waiting to pierce my skin. I was getting my ankle numbed in three separate places around the damaged area. The first shot hurt the worst every time. Shots two and three weren't too bad as I guess the numbing had already kicked in from the first shot. It took about ten minutes for my ankle to go completely numb. I remember walking to my locker feeling like a new man. I was testing my ankle by lightly jumping, speed walking and doing small cuts on the carpet. I couldn't feel anything! I literally felt like I had been given a brand-new ankle. If only it were that easy. I put on my pads and headed out with the rest of my team for pre-game warm-ups. I could run at full speed, jump at maximum height and stick my foot in the ground to run precise routes. It was amazing!

What was not so amazing was how it felt after the game as the numbness began to wear off. I could feel a tingle in my ankle and then a throb. Once the numbing completely wore off, it hurt so badly I couldn't even stand up. The pain of playing a three-hour football game on two torn tendons in my ankle literally left me useless. I couldn't move. This excruciating pain paralyzed my entire body. It hurt so badly. I pounded ibuprofen to help offset the pain, but nothing seemed to work. Walking to class on Mondays was almost impossible. I would beg people for a ride to campus to limit the distance I had to walk. When I did have to walk, I had to drag my foot. I imagine I looked like some sort of deranged zombie to my fellow classmates.

This was my new normal; my new routine for the remainder of the season. I had six weeks of ankle freedom on Saturdays, followed by a serious amount of pain throughout the remainder of the week. As a team, we didn't fare too well that season. We wrapped up with a 3-9 record, and I felt awful about it. My senior season, for the second year in a row, I was a team captain and I couldn't bring our team out of our losing slump. To this day, it wears on me that I couldn't lead our team more successfully. And I take full responsibility for my part in that. I learned that life must go on even if things don't go the way we plan for them to go. Even when we are in charge as a leader and the responsibility falls on our shoulders, we must accept the shortcoming and move forward with a positive outlook.

Although our team didn't accomplish our goal of winning a conference championship and playing in an NCAA bowl game that year, there was still a silver lining for me — the icing on the cake. I was fortunate to chase down both receiving records and leave as the University of North Texas' all-time leading receiver in career receptions and receiving yards. It had been a dream of mine for four years, and it finally came true! I was given a fancy game ball with the new reception and yardage marked to display and always cherish.

The game ball was more than just a trophy. It symbolized all the effort, hard work and sacrifice it took to leave as the school's all-time leading receiver. It was only four short years prior that I was scratching and clawing for a college scholarship and for someone to take a chance on an undersized wide receiver from McKinney, Texas. I am forever grateful for the opportunity the University of North Texas provided me. They took a chance on me by being the only division one college to offer me a scholarship.

It's funny how things come full circle. One day you are doubted, and then one day you are praised for being the best in your field. Have you experienced that feeling? Where it seems like everyone doubts you and your ability, and like me, you're hoping for that one chance, that one big break, that one opportunity that you know you're ready for? If you're in that place of uncertainty right now, let me encourage you to press through, keep pushing and fight with all your might for your opportunity. All you need is one chance and your dreams can come true. They did for me!

As that chapter of my life came to an end, I was ready for what the future had in store. But first, it was time to fix my ankle. Surgery and the path to recovery were waiting.

CHAPTER 13

8 AGENTS, 1 GOAL

"There are two types of people who will tell you that you cannot make a difference in this world: those who are afraid to try and those who are afraid you will succeed."

– Ray Goforth

ONCE MY ANKLE had healed, the next step in forging a career as a pro football player meant finding an agent. What seemed straightforward turned out to be a huge undertaking as my family, and I spoke with no less than eight potential representatives. We hadn't planned on speaking to that many, but once the process got underway, it became clear that the journey was going to be nearly as difficult and arduous as the one that led to my getting recruited for college.

The first agent we interviewed drove this really sharp looking Mercedes with a license plate that read "Super Agent." He was straight out of the movie *Jerry Maguire*, but not like Jerry himself, a good agent who fought for his clients. Instead, he was like one of the agents Jerry sought to escape, guys who were all talk and no delivery, driven by image but with little true concern for their clients. As we spoke with him, I had a feeling this was not our guy. By the time the meeting concluded, it was clear: he was *not* our guy.

We shared a meal with two lawyers from another agency. The agency paid for the meal, treating my family to dinner at an excellent upscale restaurant. But that free meal was about the only kindness they showed us. For starters, the dinner with the lawyers went three hours, which is about two hours too long for a college graduate. Their pitch was disorganized and fractured, and they seemed to think they were doing me a huge favor by even being there. But their attitude got even worse after that. They informed me that I wasn't an in-demand wide receiver, that I would be very lucky to even receive an invite to a training camp, and that I was very lucky to be talking to them for free, considering how much they normally charge per hour for "regular" clients. I couldn't wrap my mind around how arrogant they were at dinner. Once we got in the car to leave, my parents and I looked at each other and all knew immediately that they were not the group we wanted in our corner.

Finally, the tide seemed to turn. We flew to St. Louis to meet with another agency and right away, the mood, the approach and the experience felt different and much improved from the previous meetings. As my dad and I walked into their offices, a digital banner said "Welcome Johnny Quinn!" I'm not a big hype guy, but seeing that had the impression that they were hoping it would: it made me think that they genuinely wanted me or were at least interested in representing me for my professional football career. I met a few other football players on the trip that the agency was also looking to represent, and they were all nice guys. We got an inside look at where I would be training in the weeks leading up to the NFL Draft. I was feeling really good about the agency; that is, until the last day.

On the last day of my visit, we started talking logistics and what the agency's strategy would be to market me to NFL teams when the question came up of how many wide receivers they were representing for the upcoming draft. It turned out that I would be the fourth wide receiver they had under contract. Four wide receivers! Having my agency representing even one other wide receiver was an issue for me, let alone two, but three others were way too many. My heart sank as I pictured a potential scenario for the upcoming NFL draft. Think about this for a second, if this agency was in the "war room" with the Dallas Cowboys, and the Cowboys were looking for a wide receiver, how in the world could I be sure that my agency was going to sell me to the Cowboys over the other three wide receivers they also represented? The answer was, I wouldn't know. At the end of the day, as long as the agency placed a wide receiver with the Cowboys, they got paid.

If I was the person they placed, great. We would all win. If it was another receiver they represent, well, the agency would still win, but I would lose. So, although we really liked the agency and thought that they operated a first-class business, having four receivers to represent in the NFL Draft was three too many for us to give them the green light.

On our way to the airport, my dad told me that he had set up a meeting with another agency in St. Louis. During my college recruiting process in high school, I had visited Illinois State University. It turned out my dad had kept in touch with their head coach, Denver Johnson, over the years. As we had started looking for agents, he had reached out to him for advice and coach Johnson recommended that we meet his agent. Once we got to the airport, we said goodbye to the agency that brought us in and then waited in the baggage claim lobby for the next agency to send a car and pick us up!

On the ride from the airport to the new agent's offices, I kept hoping for one thing above all else: namely, that the new agency not have any other wide receivers under representation. We pulled up to a spectacular building in downtown St. Louis and rode the elevator to the top floor where the law firm had their offices. The view was sensational. We could see the iconic St. Louis Arch and the rooftops of many downtown buildings. As we sat down to go over the basics, things began to line up. I liked seeing the agent's past client representation list. I liked the way he carried himself and the proposed game plan he laid out for my future professional football-playing career. And the cherry on top was the news that they weren't representing any other wide receivers, so if we chose their group as my agency of representation, I would be the only one they would be representing for the NFL Draft! Ding, ding, ding: I think we found my agent.

We took a quick break so my dad and I could discuss, but it didn't take long for us to come to the conclusion that after eight agencies, this one was clearly the best fit! As we boarded our flight home later that evening, I was thrilled to have finally found an agent. Going through the agent selection process can be intimidating as you filter through the different egos. But now that I had an agent in place, it was time to go to work. It was time to do what I did best. It was time to prepare my body physically and mentally as I embarked on the journey to become a professional football player!

CHAPTER 14

LAST BUT *NOT* LEAST

THE 2007 NFL draft was held over two days in the "Big Apple" — New York City. Radio City Music Hall is a landmark in New York City, and the NFL draft would be taking place there during the last weekend of April. If you received an invitation as a football player to attend the NFL draft at Radio City Music Hall, then that (unofficially) meant that you were going to be a first-round draft pick. Occasionally, the board that invites the top college football prospects across the country gets it wrong and invites guests who fall into the second round. But that rarely happens. Everyone else is left watching the draft unfold on TV while clutching their cellphones in hopes of a call from an NFL team.

If you've never watched the NFL draft, the first three rounds happen on day one, while rounds four through seven happen on day two. If you happen to be the very last pick of the NFL draft at the end of round seven, you are awarded the notorious and not-so-popular title: "Mr. Irrelevant." The last pick in the NFL draft carries this title for the rest of his life, and is showered with gifts and given a special trip for being the last person on the draft board. The first person to officially be given the "Mr. Irrelevant" title was Kelvin Kirk in the 1976 NFL draft.

I was not particularly fond of the title "Mr. Irrelevant," but if having that title meant I got drafted, then I would be "Mr. Ecstatic!" My agent had been crunching the numbers and fielding phone calls from teams across the league to get an idea of where I would potentially stand come draft day. The word on the street was that my ranking placed me between a 5th round and 7th round selection; we felt good about my chances of being drafted. Of all the wide receivers declaring for the NFL draft in 2007, I was in the top 10 statistically in career reception, career yards and career touchdowns.

Things began to look brighter as we compared my statistics with other wide receivers. My agent looked at the previous nine NFL draft classes because he wanted to get an idea of roughly how many wide receivers get drafted each year into the NFL. The data from the previous nine years (1997-2006) revealed that somewhere between 28 and 32 wide receivers were drafted each year.

You don't have to be a math wiz to put those two sets of numbers together. If you are telling me that between 28 and 32 wide receivers get drafted, and my statistics put me in the top 10 of wide receivers entering that year's NFL draft, well, HURRY UP DRAFT DAY! Who's going to give me a chance and select me in the NFL draft?! Everyone in my corner was getting excited.

When draft day came, I had a small draft party at my parents' house in McKinney, Texas. Although I did not get invited to Radio City Music Hall, I still wanted to celebrate with the people closest to me. A bigger party was going to happen once I got drafted and knew which team I would be playing for in the NFL. I invited some of my closest friends and teammates from college, and we had our eyes glued to the television. My parents had food on the table for everyone, and they split their time between watching the draft on TV with us and taking phone calls from family members checking to see if I had been drafted yet. I felt a calmness in my demeanor as the draft went on and players began finding out which team they would play for. I knew it was only a matter of time before my name would be called, so I waited patiently in anticipation for that moment.

I knew I was not going to get drafted on the first day, but it was fun to watch some of the guys I played against in college see their dreams of being drafted into the NFL come true. Routinely, I would tell my friends who did not play football, "I played against that guy who just got drafted.

He was good, but if he got selected in the draft, I think I should be coming up next!"

One thing I really enjoyed doing was watching all the draft videos. Almost every time a player is drafted, the NFL Network would show a short clip of that particular player's college football highlight reel. These short draft clips were sneak peaks for all viewers watching to build excitement for the person who just got drafted. To be honest, part of me wanted to get drafted just so I could see which clips from my football career at the University of North Texas the draft committee would select.

While everyone wants to have their highlight reel played, no one wants to make someone else's draft tape. Think about that for a moment. If the NFL Network is showing a highlight reel of a college football player making a spectacular play, it had to come at someone else's expense. As the draft began to unfold, I saw that I had made someone else's draft tape. In the fourth round (112th pick), the Pittsburgh Steelers selected Daniel Sepulveda from Baylor University.

Daniel Sepulveda had won the Ray Guy Award — given to the best college punter — in both 2004 and 2006. He was a consensus first-team All-American in 2004 and a unanimous first-team All-American in 2006. Sepulveda wasn't your traditional punter either. He was a former linebacker who walked-on to the Baylor Bears before taking over shop as the team's starting punter. Most punters are not very good tacklers; it is not their responsibility. A punter's job is to punt the ball high and far, changing the field position for the team. In Sepulveda's case, he was an excellent punter but also a very good tackler, which I found out the hard way one Saturday evening in Waco, Texas.

It is always tough to play on the road, and Baylor's home field advantage was in full force. I had just scored a 68-yard touchdown (the longest of my career), so I was pretty jacked-up and ready to return a punt for a touchdown, too. I set-up on our 20-yard line and Sepulveda kicked a boomer of a punt with incredible hang time that drove me back to my 10-yard line to field his punt. I scoped out the landscape to see where my teammates were blocking as I looked ferociously for a running lane to hit. I cut left and couldn't find an opening, but then immediately cut right as

I saw a seam develop. I sprinted past the first line of defense, and could see open grass! As I began to sprint up field, a blur came in from my left side and absolutely destroyed me. I got pounded to the ground. I got de-cleated! A de-cleat is when both of your feet leave the ground as you get tackled. De-cleats are the kind of hits that are so aggressive that a crowd watching gasps and silently whispers: "I hope that person is OKAY!" That day I got de-cleated... by the punter!

Not only did my body hurt from the de-cleater, my pride took a beating too. Returners are not supposed to get tackled by the punter. It is an unwritten rule in every returner's playbook. The punter is the returner's responsibly, and the returner's job is to make the punter miss (punters are supposed to be really bad tacklers).

Sepulveda showed me and everyone in McClain Stadium that evening why he was the best punter in the country. Sepulveda went on to become one of only three people to win the Ray Guy Award twice. Ryan Allen and Tom Hackett are the other two punters to have won the award twice. Shortly after the de-cleater, my teammates helped me off the ground to gather my balance. I walked gingerly over to our sideline and immediately met our team doctors, who were waiting on me for a diagnosis.

Under my football helmet, I wear a skull cap. At the time, I had long hair and the skull cap kept my hair out of my face, so I liked wearing the caps. Sepulveda hit me so hard that when I took off my helmet, my skull cap had fallen off my head and was lying in the bottom of my helmet. This happened while the helmet was strapped on during the de-cleater. Yes, he hit me that freaking hard!

Seeing Sepulveda's hit two years after it happened on his draft tape brought back memories I wanted to forget. Now that I had made someone else's draft tape, I had a heavier sense of urgency to see my draft tape play. I wanted viewers to see and celebrate my playmaking ability, not just my de-cleater!

Things began to heat up as the draft crept into the fifth round. I received my first (and only) call from the Jacksonville Jaguars. My heart raced as I motioned to everyone in the room — *Shhh it's Jacksonville* — and the room got so quiet, you could hear a pin drop. Jacksonville's receiver coach was on the other end of the phone and said there are a few guys the team is looking at drafting in the sixth round and to be ready! I said, "Yes sir!" and waited for him to hang up the phone before jumping out of my seat and eagerly filling everyone in with the exciting news out of Jacksonville. Cheers began to erupt as people began to anticipate me getting drafted in the sixth round. My dream was almost a reality!

We studied every pick in the sixth round and held our breath as Jacksonville came on the clock. Jacksonville made their announcement as to whom they were drafting and it was not me. You could immediately feel the air sink out of the room. Everyone at my draft party pondered the Jaguar's sixth round pick and we were all confused as to why it was not me. I nodded briefly to everyone, reassuring them that everything was going to be okay and that Jacksonville had a pick in the 7th round and I would likely end up there. Dream still on!

As the last round of the NFL draft began, our eyes were glued to the television. Each pick that came on the draft board added more tension to the room after what had happened in the sixth round. Jacksonville came on the board for their final pick. We held our breath and watched the name come across the screen. It did not read Johnny Quinn. It had somebody else's name on it. I was devastated. It was like my dream had vanished into thin air.

I sat in disbelief that 254 football players had been selected in the 2007 NFL Draft and I was not one of them. Everyone at my mini-draft party was very supportive and encouraging with their comments and well wishes; the consensus among the people at my house that day was that I was going to have to do it the hard way and continue to prove people wrong — something I had been doing my entire athletic career. I agreed with their assessment and was ready to work harder than any football player on the planet. But I was also frustrated and still in shock that my dream of being drafted had not come true.

I knew after the draft that teams would begin signing free agents like crazy. It was like a free-for-all with every NFL team to get on the phone with the players on their draft board that did not get drafted and sign them to a free agent contract to get them into camp and give them a chance to earn a roster spot, just like the draft picks. Everyone knows it is harder for a free agent to make an NFL roster than it is for a draft pick. Draft picks are like college players on scholarship. The scholarship players get the opportunity to shine before the opportunity is given to the walk-ons, or in this case, the free agents. I was going to be a free agent and ready for the challenge!

It wasn't but five minutes post-draft that my agent called with some great news! I had four teams reach out and offer me free agent contracts. The Buffalo Bills, Cincinnati Bengals, New Orleans Saints and New York Jets had opportunities ready with my name on it. My agent kept a spreadsheet going during the draft on where receivers were getting drafted. It turns out 35 wide receivers were drafted (in 2007) and of the four teams that expressed interest, the Buffalo Bills were the only team that had not drafted a wide receiver.

Seeing that Buffalo had not drafted a receiver was a huge green light. It meant that the Bills would be looking to fill their final roster with a receiver or two from the free agents they signed. After ample discussion about the other three teams that showed interest, it was clear that my best opportunity to compete for a roster spot was with the Buffalo Bills. I gave my agent the nod to move forward with the Bills. It wasn't too long until the contract arrived — a three-year deal for $1.2 million. Also included was a $3,000.00 signing bonus! As I looked at the contract, my eyes beamed at the numbers. I thought — and may have said out loud — "Wow, all I have to do is play football for three years and I will get paid 1.2 million dollars? I am ready to play ball and get paid!"

After the congratulatory hugs and phone calls to out-of-state family and coaches, my mini-draft party wanted to celebrate my new team by going out to eat. We transitioned from my parents' home to a local steak house. On the drive over, we all talked about what a crazy weekend the NFL Draft had been. I could not believe I finally received a chance to live my dream of playing in the NFL. My professional career was going to start as a member of the Buffalo Bills!

Dream Back On!

CHAPTER 15

DREAM DEFERRED

"If the grass looks greener somewhere else,
it's time to water your own yard."

– Craig Groeschel

THE NEXT DAY I spoke to a Buffalo Bill's travel agent to book my flight to Buffalo, New York. I couldn't believe that my childhood dream had come true! The draft happened at the end of April, and I was scheduled to report to my new team in early May. That gave me roughly two weeks to say my goodbyes. The responses that I received from everyone were so encouraging: "I knew you would be playing in the NFL" and "ever since I saw you play in middle school, I knew you would go pro" were common responses I received from friends, family and people in the community. While it was refreshing to hear those kind words, I knew the journey was just beginning. All the work, sacrifice and dedication I had put in over the years had gotten me to the NFL, but the work wasn't over: it was time to lay it all on the line again. It was time to make my dream a reality and to cement myself as a legitimate professional football player.

When I travel, I typically make sure to pack plenty of workout gear. But this trip was different. I made sure to pack light because I knew I was about to be equipped with authentic NFL apparel. When I touched down in Buffalo, I headed towards the baggage claim area and that's when I saw my ride. The driver held up a sign that read, "The Buffalo Bills welcome Johnny Quinn." It was so cool seeing my name on that sign! I grabbed my luggage, jumped in the car and headed to Orchard Park, New York. I was a bit confused about our destination until I realized that Ralph Wilson Stadium and the Buffalo Bills are located right outside of Buffalo in Orchard Park, New York.

Our first stop was to the stadium for physicals. Professional football teams want an immediate "look-over" by their team physicians. This involves poking and prodding, testing the movement of each joint and ligament to make sure everything looks good and strong. If you think about their reasoning behind immediate physicals for newly acquired football players, it makes logical sense. The team wants to make sure that they are getting their money's worth for each player. I received the green light and walked into the locker room to find my locker.

I found my locker, and it was as if time came to a complete standstill. I thought to myself: *Wow, there is my name "QUINN" in an NFL locker room!* I don't know how long I stared in astonishment, but I made sure to embrace the moment. A few other players started to make their way into the locker room, breaking my concentration. I quickly settled into my locker, and acting like I owned the place, I began to unpack the few items

I brought with me. The Bills put the rookies in a side locker room, which is pretty standard for most teams in the NFL, but I didn't care. It was only going to be a matter of time until I was in the official locker room. I tried on all my gear to make sure everything fit properly. I purposely walked the long way to the equipment room to take a few quick (or not so quick) glances of myself in my new gear in the bathroom mirror. There was no question that if someone were paying close attention, they would have known exactly what I was doing. But whether anyone was watching me or

Catching a pass during rookie mini-camp

not, I don't think I would have cared. I was soaking in the experience of putting on my NFL gear for the first time!

We had a few days to get acclimated before our rookie mini-camp began. A rookie mini-camp is essentially a crash course of the playbook to help get the new guys up to speed before practicing with the veterans. Our camp spanned the course of three days. Each of those days, the coaches had us practicing twice a day. These camps are also a time for management to bring in free agents on a tryout basis. Essentially, a team signs a free agent to a three-day contract before deciding if they want to extend the contract or part ways. In most cases, teams and three-day contract guys separate after the three-day workout.

Rookies were hungry to showcase their skills and start chipping away at a starting spot on the roster. The top three draft picks for the Buffalo Bills were running back Marshawn Lynch (California), linebacker Paul Posluszny (Penn State) and quarterback Trent Edwards (Stanford). I made sure to warm up with Trent, and I noticed a particular zip on all his throws. Wow, he could really hum the ball in there. I quickly made a mental note to get my hands and eyes up early when running passing routes with him.

The rookie mini-camp went very well; a lot of plays and a lot of studying took place. We didn't have much time to prepare before taking the field with the veterans. After studying the playbook and thumbing through all the plays, I came to a realization that I had never considered before. I grew up watching football on Sundays and listening to commentators talk about how smart football players needed to be due to the sheer size of the playbook and number of plays it offers. While I do agree the size and plays are ample, I started to see very familiar concepts. Three step slant. Five step stop. Nine is the number that signifies a deep route, also known as a fade route. What I came to realize is that those were all routes I had learned and ran successfully in middle school football. Actually, I had been running those routes for years! See, I was under the impression that when I got to the pros, I would be running double move routes and trick plays. I mean isn't that what professionals were supposed to do? Run the tough stuff and super fun double moves? Although the complex routes were available in the playbook, we didn't turn to them very often. Instead, we focused on the basics. Three steps, five steps, nine route. We worked on mastering the basics by running them over and over again.

Now I want you to think about that in your profession. How often are we under the assumption that as we climb the ladder of success, we must learn the double moves and tough stuff because that is what we will be doing at the top? When in all actuality, what we need to do is master the basics. It is important to understand that the fundamentals are what make a difference so that we can be consistent every day and on every play. Whether the sun is out or it is raining, we must be consistent. It doesn't matter if we have money in the bank or if we are broke, or whether our spouse, kids, or friends are in a good mood or in an awful mood. The key is to always be a student of the game and master the fundamentals. Sure, there will be time for double moves and trick plays. Just like there will be time for hard decisions and strategic moves. But the great ones in life understand that it's a mastering of the fundamentals and being able to deliver them day in and day out regardless of our circumstances. This is the secret sauce of what separates the pretenders from the contenders. Let's choose to be a contender!

Team practice began with the rookies and veterans, and we were off to a fast start. On day three of OTAs (off-season training activities), we were running routes "on air." Routes "on air" are when the quarterbacks and the wide receivers work together against no defense. We run the plays we want to work on for the day together, with no one else on the field. After routes on air, we join the defense in practice to see if the routes will work against live defenders. My first route was a post. I was called to explode off the line with speed and on my fourth outside step, plant my foot in the ground and explode up field at a 45-degree angle towards the goal post (hence the name "post route"). My hands are relaxed, the quarterback snaps the ball and I am off the line with speed. One step outside, two steps outside, three steps outside, as I count in my head like clockwork. It's time to plant my foot on the fourth outside step and explode up field at 45-degrees. I plant and explode! Something exploded all right, but unfortunately, it wasn't me towards the goal post. Nope, instead, it was my right hamstring. I can't continue with any speed whatsoever. I come to a stop as my hamstring is throbbing like crazy and feels like it is tied into a massive knot. I can't make the pain go way. It gets worse, and now I can't even move my leg. Not knowing what to do because I haven't had this feeling before, I hobble over to the sideline and sit down. The pain won't go away and I look helplessly at my right leg wondering when it's going to stop. The training staff saw everything and jogged over to offer relief. "Looks like a hamstring," the team doctor said immediately. "Well, I don't know what it is," I told him, "but I can't move my right leg. There is a knot back there, and it hurts." I pointed to the back of my leg where my hamstring is located. The doctor motioned to my coach signaling that I was done for the day and we headed into the training room for a more thorough and proper diagnosis.

Come to find out, I had pulled my right hamstring. The "pop" I felt running the post route was when I tore my hamstring, which sent my body into shut down mode to protect the muscle from doing even more damage. There are different degrees of hamstring injuries, where the most severe requires surgery. Thankfully it wasn't that bad, but it wasn't a minor tear either. After being examined by the team doctor and medical staff, they estimated my timeline of recovery was four to six weeks. I immediately thought to myself, "You have got to be kidding me, a pulled hamstring on day three?" By this time, I was laying on the training table with ice tightly packed around my hamstring to reduce as much swelling as possible. I couldn't believe this was happening to me at such a crucial point in my professional football career. I ran four years of division one college track and never had a hamstring injury, but day three of my childhood dream, for this to happen, it just didn't seem fair.

The NFL is an acronym for National Football League. As players, we also joke that it stands for Not For Long, and that particular acronym proved to be true. This was the first time someone actually told me to my face that I wasn't good enough. Who knows, maybe people have said that about me before, but no one has told me that to my face. The team didn't want to keep me around, let me rehabilitate my hamstring and make a run at the roster. They didn't believe I added value to their team. It was tough to hear those words. I didn't like the feeling of not measuring up and the feeling of being worthless. Right then and there, the Buffalo Bills cut me. Contract lost. Dream deferred.

CHAPTER 16

LAMBEAU LEAP

*"There's winning and there's losing and in life both will happen.
What is never acceptable to me is quitting."*

– Earvin "Magic" Johnson

GETTING CUT FROM the Buffalo Bills was very hard emotionally. It was the first time someone said I wasn't good enough to help the team win. I didn't know how to process that. It just didn't register with my brain. Up until that point, I had found success as a football player, overcoming the odds, understanding the importance of working hard, yet it wasn't enough for the Bills to keep me on the roster. Coming back to Texas as a failure, or so I thought, was difficult. Mostly because I had no idea what I would do. I knew I needed to continue to train, but I knew I also needed to find work if I was going to continue to pursue my dream.

I liked working out, so naturally, I was drawn to training other people, helping them achieve their fitness goals. I took a three-day personal training course at the Cooper Aerobic Center in Dallas, Texas, which would satisfy the requirements to becoming a personal trainer. The founder of Cooper Aerobics is Dr. Kenneth Cooper, who has been referred to as the "Father of Aerobics." That's because his research in the early 80's proved to be groundbreaking in the aerobic training field. He is known for the Cooper Mile, which is a test where you see just how quickly you can run or walk 1.5 miles.

The personal training course went by smoothly, and it was fun participating in some of the coaching drills and techniques I learned during that time. Once I received my certificate, I immediately headed over to a newly built gym in my city, L.A. Fitness. It was about a ten-minute drive from my house, which made it reasonably easy to get to and from the gym in between clients. I liked the idea of building my own schedule. That was until I saw my first paycheck. It was only a few months ago that I had signed a three-year contract for $1.2 million with the Buffalo Bills, and here I was only making $12 an hour as a personal trainer. Now please understand that I don't have a problem with hard work, as that was my foundation for making it from the Texas high school football field to an NFL team, but $12 an hour just wasn't going to cut it. I had big dreams for my life, and at that rate per hour, I couldn't see myself attaining my goals anytime soon. I will say that one thing that was worth more than money was the relationships I built with a few of my clients. It was extremely gratifying to see their lives transformed, pound by pound. To be a small part of their life change was phenomenal, and that feeling of satisfaction filled my heart. Although that part was rewarding, I was still picking up the pieces of my heart from my dream being temporarily put on hold.

It seemed like years, but it had only been a few months since that dreadful day in Buffalo when I got cut. I had been in constant communication with my agent since then to see if he had any new leads. Every week I was watching the NFL rosters to see who was getting benched, cut, injured and released, paying close attention to the receiver position, hoping for another opportunity to showcase my skills. November came around that year and I finally received the call I was looking for from my agent. The Green Bay Packers had reached out and requested a tryout to see if I was in shape and how I had healed from my hamstring injury back in the spring. The call came in on a Friday, and I was on a plane to Green Bay, Wisconsin the following Monday for a private workout with my potential future employer.

If you haven't been to the Packers' Lambeau Field, I strongly encourage you to add it to your bucket list. Driving up to the field I saw this gigantic "G" located at the top of the stadium that I am sure is visible to onlookers from miles away. What I found particularly interesting was that Lambeau

Field was built in the middle of a neighborhood, surrounded by lots of houses. That's right, on the other side of the street were homes, making the field feel just like it was part of the community. How cool would that be to have Lambeau Field right next door? Maybe that's why the Packers' fans are so passionate about the green and gold. The Green Bay Packers are the only team in the NFL that does not have a traditional owner. Instead, the Packers are owned by their fans. The fans are the shareholders and are considered the owner of the team. It's a pretty cool concept, and it ignites the passion of the entire state of Wisconsin and other Packer faithful around the country.

It was a brisk morning in Green Bay during my workouts; you better believe they made me run routes and do the football testing drills outside to see how I handled the cold. The workout went very well. I caught every single pass that was thrown my way. The Packers brought in former LSU quarterback Rohan Davey for the tryout as well, so we made sure to work well together in hopes of us both leaving with a contract that day. After wrapping up a strong performance, both Rohan and I were told we had an hour to get showered and dressed before heading back to the airport. Despite a great showcase, I was heading back to Texas without a contract. The flight home felt twice as long as I pondered what was next. I was confused because my workout went great, yet the Packers chose not to sign me. The last words I heard from Green Bay management were that they would be in touch with my agent.

Christmas came that year and the NFL season was starting to wrap up. Only the top teams would continue to the playoffs while most of the other teams, who weren't going to be playing playoff football, would start to build their rosters for the next season. I remember watching the first playoff game just after the New Year when the Green Bay Packers played the New York Giants in a chilly contest on the frozen tundra of Lambeau Field. As the camera crew would span to aerial shots of the stadium in between plays, I could see the fields where my tryout was conducted only two short months previously. The Packers ended up losing to the New York Giants. I don't know if anyone knew at the time, besides Brett Favre himself, but that ended up being his last game as a Green Bay Packer. The

New York Giants went on to beat the undefeated New England Patriots in Super Bowl XLII. That game was electric. It was during that game, the New York Giants receiver, David Tyree, had an amazing one-handed catch where he braced the football against his helmet.

A day after Green Bay's loss to the Giants, I received the break I had been praying for: the Packers scouting department called my agent to offer a futures contract. What that meant was that I would sign right then and there, in early January, and report to my new team in March when the official off-season began for the Packers. I was so excited! This was just the opportunity I needed to prove myself and show that I could play in the National Football League. I signed another three-year contract, this time for $1.4 million.

Thankfully, I was already in shape due to the potential for free agent workouts. I knew at any time, my agent could call with a request from a potential employer who wanted to see my skills, so I made sure to stay game-ready. After signing my new deal with the Green Bay Packers, I had two months to fine-tune my skills before I reported to snowy Green Bay, Wisconsin. In Texas, winter basically ends in January, so I can't say that my upbringing really prepared me for the cold I was about to experience. Driving into Green Bay, I realized that I better get used to the cold quickly. There was snow everywhere.

As an undrafted free agent, the Packers put me in a hotel close to Lambeau Field. It was an extended stay hotel and players would come and go. My plan was to punch a ticket on the final roster, which would give me the freedom to move out of the hotel and find a permanent location in cozy Green Bay. Although my room in the extended stay hotel was small, there were benefits: fresh towels, a clean room and warm chocolate chip cookies in the lobby every day at 4:00 PM. As strong as I was in the weight room, I was even stronger in the sweet tooth department. My love of sweets commands some serious attention. I may have even set up a notification on my phone to alert me at 3:55 PM that the fresh batch of cookies were on their way out of the oven and into the lobby.

My first day during off-season training with the Packers had us in the weight room where we began to establish a lifting chart. At the professional level, strength coaches typically take the first week at the beginning of the season of the lifting program to assess the strength and mobility of each athlete to help customize the most efficient and effective program. While some of the pros took the off-season to rest and recover, I didn't have that luxury, so I reported to the Packers weight room strong and in excellent shape. I set some very good numbers that day, but the end of the workout is what I remember the most. In the Green Bay weight room, there is an area where athletes can make protein shakes, grab fruit, snacks, bars, and just about anything else you could think of or want. They had everything you need to refuel after a grueling workout. They even had this giant refrigerator with protein drinks you grab right off the shelf. I'm pretty sure they had every flavor known to man. As I stared at the massive amount of options, one of the veteran players came over to introduce himself. His name was Aaron Rodgers, and he was slated to start at quarterback now that Brett Favre made the announcement he was retiring. "Hey man, what's your name, where are you from, what do you like to do?" he asked. I said, "My name is Johnny Quinn, I am from Texas and I like to play Halo."

Halo is a first-person shooter game on Xbox. Confession: I am a little bit of a nerd when it comes to video games. In college, I was on a team that competed at Major League Gaming's National Halo Tournament where we placed in the top 16 in the nation. My gamer tag (Xbox name) is Yoda, and it would be common to hear my teammates call me Yoda in the locker room and around campus. They knew I took my Halo playing very seriously. Aaron said he played Halo too and wanted to see if I wanted to come over and play with him. Do you know that feeling you get when you meet someone for the first time and hit it off so well it feels as if you have been friends for years? Well, that's how I felt, and I was just glad that I found someone to play Halo with during breaks and in-between practices. I was pleased to make my first friend in Green Bay. I went to grab a protein shake out of the fridge, and I must have hit the shelf by accident with my hand as the entire top row came crashing down, knocking all the protein shakes out of the refrigerator and onto the floor. To say I was embarrassed would be a gross understatement. I was mortified and immediately looked at Aaron and surveyed the weight room to see if there were any other onlookers for the catastrophe I just created. Aaron chuckled and then joined me as part of the cleanup crew, placing the protein shakes back on the shelf. Great! My first day in the Green Bay Packers facility and I knock over all the protein shakes. I wondered to myself what day two had in store as I replayed the horror of all those protein shakes crashing to the floor.

I met Aaron before he became an NFL MVP and Super Bowl Champion. He's a guy who has set, and will continue to set, multiple NFL records. Some say he may become the greatest quarterback the NFL has ever seen. Aaron will one day be inducted into the NFL Hall of Fame, and that will be an honor that is well deserved. One thing I can say with complete confidence and accuracy is that Aaron is as genuine and authentic of a person as I have ever met. His words and actions align, and that's something you don't find that much these days, especially with the level of success and notoriety he has obtained. His friendship helped me pave the way for a strong off-season — and a run at making the final roster once we got into August when teams began to make cuts.

Leading up to the pre-season, things in Green Bay went very well. People came and went, but I remained a constant. I steadily began to work my way into the huddle and was even selected as off-season performer of the week, an award given each week during the off-season to a player who demonstrates excellence and what it takes to wear the green and gold. Things were really starting to line up, and I couldn't wait until pre-season football began. Our first game was on Monday Night Football, at home in historic Lambeau Field versus the Cincinnati Bengals. Putting on my uniform, standing in the tunnel before running out into Lambeau with 70,000+ Packer faithful fans cheering loudly was truly unbelievable. I remember it like it was yesterday. I journeyed back in my mind to running through a makeshift banner at McKinney High School, the tunnel helmet at the University of North Texas and the demand and sacrifice it took to become the best football player I could possibly become and it all led me to this moment.

As I sat there in the tunnel of Lambeau Field, embracing the moment, listening to the roaring fans, a question popped up in my mind. Was it worth it? Was it worth the struggle to walk onto the track team in college and take last place for two years? Was it worth believing that I could play in the NFL even though I was 5'11 and 7/8ths, my official recorded height? Was it worth the physical and mental demand football, or really anything in life you want to accomplish, takes? I can answer all of these questions with an emphatic, YES! At that particular moment in time, it finally all made sense. I understood what all the dedication, commitment and pursuit of excellence meant, and it was totally worth it.

I don't know where you are today in your journey as you read this book. Maybe you're in the messy middle, where things are tough and you can't see past tomorrow. I just want to encourage you and let you know that if you're asking the very same question I did, "is it worth it?" then the answer is yes. Do me a favor and continue to put one foot in front of the other and press forward. Maybe you need to revisit the "why" in your journey. By that I mean, maybe you need to remember why you began going after your dreams in the first place. Although at this moment things may be cloudy and the vision may look blurry, I need you to know that the reward at the end is so much greater than your current hurdle or struggle.

The starters for Green Bay played the first few series, but then it was time to see what the rookies and free agents had in their tank. My first play from scrimmage was a run play, and I made a point to show the guy guarding me that it was going to be a long night for him. In college, we had such talented running backs that I did a lot of blocking. I took pride in being a good blocker, where traditionally, wide receivers aren't known for their blocking. I wanted the defensive back for the Cincinnati Bengals to know that it was going to be a very physical night, so get ready my friend. We ran a few more plays, a couple runs and passes, but still no action my way. But whether the ball came my way or not, you can be sure I was determined to execute with the utmost effort I could possibly exert.

Midway through the third quarter, Matt Flynn, Green Bay's 7th round selection, came in at the quarterback position. The coordinator called a play action pass where Matt would fake a handoff to the running back, with the hopes of drawing the defense up and out of position, so we could throw a deep pass. I was on the opposite side of where the play was going, and my responsibility on this particular pass was to book it across the field with speed to get in Matt's line of sight in the event the deep ball wasn't open. When I say I accelerated off the ball with speed, I mean it was like I was shot out of a cannon. I wasn't going to miss a chance to be in the quarterback's line of fire. And sure enough, Matt looked deep, didn't like his options and then adjusted his eyesight to where we immediately locked eyes; I instantly knew the trigger was about to be pulled. I could feel the defender breathing down my neck, so it was imperative that I kept the pedal to the medal and not slow down. Matt would have to throw the ball in front of me so we wouldn't risk a deflection, or worse, an interception. By this time, my momentum had not only carried me across the field of play to get in Matt's line of vision, but I was rapidly approaching the sideline. I saw the ball released and tracked it down with laser focus. As I extended my hands to bring the ball in, the defender wrapped one arm around my waist and tried to disrupt the ball with his other arm. As I felt him tackle me, I did not give him a chance to get his arm in between my hands and the ball. I had a death grip on that pigskin. I kept both feet in bounds as our momentum carried us into the sideline and right into a few of my teammates. We both were like a bowling ball, and they were the pins. I don't think it was a strike, but we still cleared a decent amount of space. I had that ball latched in my hands so tightly; no one was going to take it from me. My concern now was, did the referee call it a catch for being in bounds? As I cranked my neck to find a visual of the ref, I saw him motion with both hands that it was a catch and I was in bounds. FIRST DOWN!

We came up short that Monday night, but if you looked at my face or had a conversation with me after the game, you would have thought we won the Super Bowl! I was on cloud nine after securing my first NFL reception, on Monday Night Football, in historic Lambeau Field. I would have to soak up all the emotion and memories from my first NFL game that night, because it was back to business the following day. Next, we had two away games, which took us to Denver, Colorado to play the Broncos and San Francisco, California to play the 49ers.

As a young receiver growing up and climbing through the ranks of middle school football, I was, and still am today, a huge Jerry Rice fan! Jerry has just about every major receiver record in the NFL and some experts argue he is the best football player of all time. There is no doubt he is the best receiver of all time. During pre-game warm-up in Candlestick Stadium, I was in awe that this was the exact field that Jerry Rice, Joe Montana and the dominant 49ers of the 1990's had played on.

About midway through the 3rd quarter, we had a run play called that would send the running back my way. It was imperative that I blocked my defender to try and create an open hole for our running back on the out-side. I could feel the steam of the pile moving my way, and I dug my feet into the trenches as I braced to keep the guy guarding me away from our running back. The pile was now directly behind me, engulfing my legs from the back and bending me backwards over the pile. Someone had swung their body into the back of my legs without warning, flipping me helplessly onto the pile. It was one of those plays where people watching on TV say, "Ouch! I hope he is okay." It felt awful getting rolled up from behind, and I immediately limped off the field for the training staff to evaluate my leg that had just done the equivalent of a gymnastic backbend.

We headed into the locker room for further examination and boy had I sure dodged a bullet. I had a few scrapes on my calf and a quarter sized bruise on my ankle. Now that my adrenaline had cooled off, I knew once I stood up and put pressure on my leg that it would collapse. I gin-gerly moved off the table and placed my healthy leg on the ground first to establish a strong base before I tested my other leg. To everyone's surprise, including mine, I was able to put pressure, stand and walk without any restrictive range of motion. The Charlie Horse from the bruise in my calf didn't feel too hot, but boy did I get lucky. There was nothing restrictive that would keep me out of our last pre-season football game. I didn't even have to miss any practice time.

One of the neat things about flying as a team is having a private plane. In college, we flew Southwest Airlines and had to check in at the terminal, just like everyone else. We had the plane to ourselves, but had to go to the gate for scheduled departure and follow all the proper boarding procedures. In the NFL, it's totally different. It is so much cooler! Delta brought in an international plane to Green Bay for us to charter to away games. Have you been on an international flight or seen those types of planes? They are mas-sive! Needless to say, we had plenty of room. Players were taking up entire rows and lying down. It was the best. No one had a middle passenger. We didn't even have to turn off our large electronics for takeoff. Once we cleared 10,000 feet and it was okay for the flight attendants to start drink service, one of our options was milk and cookies. You know my ears perked when I heard that. I couldn't believe all the options we had on our flight and was certain to take advantage of the unlimited supply of chocolate chip cookies! Flying in the NFL felt like the best field trip of all time.

Leading up to the last game of the pre-season, I felt the pressure intensify as this was when the final roster cuts were made, and I saw a few of my buddies go home. The roster was at 85 players, and they had to trim it down to 75. Ten of my teammates, mostly new players in the NFL, but a few veterans, were cut after the third game. It's always tough to see your buddies leave, not knowing if your paths will ever cross again. You also don't know if you're going to be the next to go. It's quite the mind game and if you're not careful, you start second-guessing every decision, thinking you are the next to get cut. And that's a bad spot to be in mentally. I knew I had one more game to showcase my skills and make a run at the final roster. We were playing the Tennessee Titans at home in Lambeau, and the final pre-season game is when the rookies and players who haven't established a name for themselves, get most of the playing time. It's our last audition before final cuts. This cut is the biggest one where each team has to trim the roster down by 22 players, to create a 53-man roster. It's a big cut!

I played very well that night. I blocked my tail off and caught two short slant routes to help move the chains. For my non-football friends who are reading this book, moving the chains means to get a first down. A first down is when — never mind, you know what I'm trying to say. We were down by a touchdown and a last-second throw to the end zone went to another rookie free-agent wide receiver. I was overwhelmed with joy that we scored as time ran out. At the same time, I couldn't help but think that spectacular play landed him a spot on the final roster. In a regular season game, the correct and safe call is to kick the extra point and head to overtime. With final cuts looming in the near distance, head coach Mike McCarthy chose to go for the riskier move. He wanted to go for the 2-point conversion and secure the win.

Matt Flynn was behind center and called the final play. I was the inside receiver in the slot on the left-hand side and my route was to run a flag route. A flag route is when you push up field and head to the corner of the end zone. Or in other words, it's the opposite of running a post route, where you run towards the goal post. My responsibility was to beat my defender with speed, get open and let the quarterback throw me the ball. As Matt called the snap count, I took a quick glance to see where the defensive back was lined up. He was off and inside, set up perfectly for me to run a flag route. I looked back at the line of scrimmage and knew Matt was coming my way with the football. I exploded off the line when the ball was snapped, planted my foot in the ground and make a beeline for the corner of the end zone. I arched my head back, and sure enough, I saw the football heading my way. I knew I had to step on the gas as I saw he placed a perfect throw towards the corner of the end zone. As I jumped to secure the ball at the highest point (players are taught that in peewee football), the defender pushed me towards the sideline while I was in midair. I caught the football, but my momentum and the extra shove from the defensive back only allowed me to get one foot in the end zone. At the time, in the pros, you needed two feet in for a reception to be called complete. Even if you were being pushed out of bounds in midair. They have since changed the rule to state that if a receiver is pushed out of bounds while in the air, it is considered a catch. I looked at the official, and sure enough, he signaled no catch, game over and we lost to the Titans by one point.

The guys in the locker room were very encouraging, but I knew I needed that play to count in order to help my case for a roster spot. After the post-game speech from our head coach, we received word that the final cut would be made between 8:00 AM and 9:00 AM so we were to stay by our phones in the morning. I don't know how much sleep I got that night, but I remember just replaying the final play over and over in my mind, trying to imagine what I could have done differently to get both feet in bounds.

I was up early the next day, went down to the lobby to grab the continental breakfast I was now used to getting every morning for the last eight months and headed back up to my room to watch the clock. When 8:00

AM showed up on my hotel clock, I immediately looked at my phone for it to ring. At 8:05 AM my phone continued to remain silent. At 8:15 AM I started pacing in my room, looking outside the window, watching a few of my teammates get in the car and head to the stadium. I knew exactly where they were going. They got the call to come in, turn in their playbook and pack up their gear. At 8:30 AM it was so quiet in my room; you could hear a pin drop. At this point, I was 50% surprised I hadn't been called, and 50% excited that I was about to make my first NFL roster! Then the clock turned to 8:32 AM and my phone rang. It was a number I hadn't seen before, but I was all too familiar with the area code of 920: Green Bay, Wisconsin. I answered the phone slowly and said hello with a shallow voice in the hopes that it was a wrong number. Well it wasn't; I received the call to come to the locker room, grab my playbook and clean out my locker.

I was devastated on the drive over to Lambeau Field, as I knew this was my final hurrah with this historic program. I headed up to the coach's office and first met with my receiver coach Jimmy Robinson. As I write this chapter, it has been seven years since I got cut from Green Bay and I still remember walking into coach Robinson's office and hearing him listen to classical music softly on his computer as we sat down for my exit interview. I always liked coach Robinson, and I don't remember much of what he said as I was trying my hardest to hold back the tears I could feel forming. Football players don't cry remember? Yeah, right! My next stop was to coach Mike McCarthy's office, and he had some really kind words to say about my style of play as wide receiver. He mentioned how he liked how physical I was and how much pride I took in my blocking. Although it was a compliment, I was getting cut now for the second time, and the pain and emotional agony was overwhelming. It felt awful. I could feel my lip began to quiver, which meant tears were on the brink of spilling over, so I immediately stood up to shake his hand and walk out which helped delay my tears.

I was in Green Bay the same year they drafted Jordy Nelson in the second round. What a spectacular player he has become! I loved seeing his work ethic during my short stint with the Packers. Also drafted that year, was Brett Swain in the 7th round. As I walked into the football administration office to get my papers, I was surprised to see Brett sitting there with a sad look on his face. They cut Brett, me and three other free-agent wide receivers. Jordy was the only one to make the final roster. I was still pretty upset and began pondering who exactly they were keeping for the practice squad. I knew if Jordy was the only new receiver they kept for the final roster, surely they would have to keep one or two receivers for the practice squad. The four newly-cut receivers and I were sitting in the football office when they announced that Brett and another receiver were the Packers practice squad selections. I immediately turned my head to the ground and closed my eyes trying to erase the day from my memory.

As everyone stood up and started to exit the office, the Green Bay official pulled me aside and said, "Hey, we want to keep you in Green Bay for 24 hours in the event Brett and/or Jake get picked up on waivers, you are our next guy in line for the practice squad." Once you get cut from an NFL team, you have 24 hours to clear waivers. What that means is another team checks the waiver board a.k.a. the cut list and can get first dibs on picking up newly-cut players. Once the 24-hour window passes, then each football player is free to sign with any team he wants.

When I received the news that I would be staying in Green Bay for one more day, I felt a small glimmer of hope creep back into my heart. I was praying so hard that one of the receivers would be claimed off of waivers and I would continue to build my career in Green Bay, Wisconsin. I have to admit, that day was tough. I came back to my hotel and started crying like a big baby. I had an excuse with the Buffalo Bills. They cut me because of my hamstring injury, so I felt as though that situation was out of my control. Now I was with the Green Bay Packers and things were different. I was playing good football and made a strong push at the final roster, but it still wasn't enough. I woke up the next morning to receive the news that neither receiver was claimed off of waivers. I packed my bag and headed to the airport for my final flight back to Texas. My second NFL contract was now terminated, and my dream of playing in the NFL was now over.

CHAPTER 17

FOOTBALL PURGATORY

"There are no secrets to success. It is the result of preparation, hard work and learning from failure."

–Colin Powell

OUCH, THAT HURT. I had now been cut twice, so you would think I would be getting used to the feeling. This was something different though; a different feeling altogether. See, in Buffalo, I didn't get a fair shot. I tore my hamstring and that was it — the Bills management wrote me off entirely. I think knowing that I didn't get a fair shot soothed my nerves the first time. It numbed the pain of getting cut. It was a distraction. But the second time getting cut was totally different. This time I received a fair shot. As a matter of fact, I played football to the best of my ability and it wasn't enough to win the Packers' management over and reserve a roster spot with my name on it.

As I moped around Texas, trying to figure out the next step in the pursuit of my dream, I kept coming up with nothing. My future in football seemed dim. I thought to myself *It's over, maybe it's time to hang up the cleats and move on. Sure, that time comes for every football player, and I have been fortunate to make it this far.* Do you see the mind games I was playing? I think if we're honest with ourselves, we all play these sorts of mind games when things get tough. I started justifying this crappy situation that I was in, instead of embracing failure and seeing where it could ultimately springboard me.

I received a call from my agent two weeks after returning from Green Bay and thought to myself as I was picking up the phone, *Wow, that was fast, another team!* Well, it was another team all right, the San Jose Sharks of Arena I Football wanted to bring me in for a workout. One of their scouts happened to be in Green Bay scouting the "leftovers" during the pre-season and must have passed my name along to San Jose staff. I remember flying out to San Jose and stepping into their locker room for the first time. I don't think it's a San Jose thing, I think it's an Arena Football thing, but their facilities were in bad shape. Mismatched weights in the weight room, lockers falling apart. Talk about doing a full 180 going from the Green Bay Packers Lambeau — and its top of the line amenities — to the bottom of the barrel.

There were a handful of receivers in for a tryout — all of us had come from an NFL camp where we received the pink slip to head home, so the talent was pretty strong across the board. I had a great workout, caught the ball very well but had a tough time getting used to the waggle motion. If you have ever watched Arena Football, the wide receivers get a head start. They can run behind the line, towards the line of scrimmage and at various angles. It's a crazy thing to watch on TV or in person, and it's even crazier to run routes with this waggle motion. I struggled on the waggle. Who knows if that played a part in my not receiving a contract to join the San Jose team? So, there I was on another flight back to Texas with the same outcome. No contract, no dream. I knew football was over at that point if I couldn't even make an Arena team. No offense to any Arena Football players out there.

I began to embark on the "What do you want to do with your life" journey. I had no idea. I liked training, I liked working out, but being a personal trainer was not my calling. I did have a few of my college coaches reach out to me about coaching; asking if that was something I would con-sider. Quite frankly, it crossed my mind a lot. To break into coaching at the collegiate level, typically, you start out as a graduate assistant, also known as a G.A. It's like being a freshman in college all over again: no money, Ramen Noodles for food… you get the idea. The one nice thing is the university does pay for graduate assistants to get their Master's degree. That's just about the only icing on the cake: the Ramen Noodle cake. I almost bit on the coaching gig, but felt like I still could play ball and needed to exhaust all my options there so I would never look back with regrets. Although I didn't really have any options left, I kept thinking my agent would call with another opportunity.

Dreaming can be fun, but it doesn't pay the bills, so I had to figure something out quickly. I spoke to my dad, and one of his first jobs after college was selling insurance. He told me I could make a "pretty penny" selling life insurance, so I said, "sign me up!" I took the required test to sell term and whole life insurance and hit the road. By road, I mean hit the phone book. There were some pretty awkward calls as a newbie insurance agent, but I started to get a knack for it and began consuming any and all books on how to sell. I still remember selling my first insurance policy. It landed me a hefty commission. I divided my commission check by my hourly wage as a personal trainer, and it came out to like a gazillion hours I would have had to work to match this commission check. *Not bad*, I thought. I can do this. I don't particularly enjoy it, but I can certainly do this to make ends meet as I continue to go after my dream as a professional football player!

At this time, a new league was forming: the AAFL, known as the All-American Football League. It had a very interesting concept. In order to be eligible to play in this league, you had to be a college graduate. You had to have your degree. If you don't know this by now, there is quite the stereotype with football players. The stereotype basically says football players only go to school to play football, that's it. What is unfortunate is that statistics across the board support this claim: football players have some of the worst graduation rates of any athletes.

I had to drive to Arkansas for this tryout with the AAFL, and it was a total crapshoot. All you had to do was pay $100, show that you graduated from college and you could try out. There were guys out there who were 10 years removed from their playing days. Here's the deal — unless you're Brett Favre, if you have grey hair, you shouldn't be at a football tryout as a potential athlete. I remember testing the pro-agility drill which tests lateral movement of an athlete, and a few of the, let's say, *older* contestants, didn't even have cleats on. They were slipping and sliding all over the place.

My workout went very well; I caught all the balls thrown my way and as the tryout came to a conclusion, I received a verbal agreement that someone from their staff would be in touch. To this day, I still have never heard from them, and I don't think the AAFL ever took off. It's probably a good thing that I didn't either. Can you imagine those bloopers and not-top-10 plays Sports Center would be running? Too funny!

One of my teammates from Green Bay was a quarterback who graduated from West Texas A&M. After his stint with the Packers, he headed north to the Canadian Football League and was a member of the Saskatchewan Roughriders. I would see his posts on social media from time to time, which piqued my interest as I was dying to play organized football as soon as possible. I reached out to him, asking how he liked it and if they needed any receivers as I was still in the market for a playing position. Shortly after my inquiry with my buddy, the general manager of the Roughriders reached out to my agent and offered a two-year contract. During that time frame, I was exploring all of my options in the CFL and reached out to one of my former college teammates at the University of North Texas who was now playing with the Hamilton Tiger-Cats. He was a defensive back turned linebacker in the pros and was making a strong name for himself in the Canadian Football League. After a back and forth conversation on playing time, life adjustment and what it's like playing ball in Canada, the general manager for the Tiger-Cats sent my agent a two-year contract as well.

I now had two CFL contracts on the table and finally had some options. I thought the timing was very interesting, as the contracts came in roughly one week apart. As we were considering both contracts, one of the key deciding factors was analyzing the current wide receivers on each roster. My agent, family and I thought my best chance to earn a roster spot and playing time was in Saskatchewan. It was also good to see the Roughriders were only a few years removed from their last Grey Cup Championship, which is the CFL's version of the Super Bowl. I made my decision to sign with the Saskatchewan Roughriders and finally had a place to call my new football home. Fortunately, I had some time to get ready before reporting to training camp. I signed with the Roughriders in December and didn't have to report until June. The contract I signed secured my rights to the team, meaning I couldn't go to another team, or even to an NFL team. I was locked in. Some players are not happy to give away that right, but considering the position I was in, I was just thankful to have another opportunity.

Having six months to prepare for my new opportunity was actually a blessing. I could finally format my training for an upcoming season. The past two years, getting cut, I had to stay in football "testing" shape. At any time, my agent could call with a workout, and it would be imperative that my testing numbers were outstanding. I always had to stay ready to run a 40-yard dash. In order to accomplish outstanding testing numbers, I had to control some of my weight room programming so it wouldn't leave me too sore in the event a phone call came in the next day. While running a fast 40-yard dash and having great testing numbers were crucial for a new contract, staying in that kind of shape isn't ideal because of the grind your body takes throughout a full season. It's critically important to build a strong foundation in the off-season months that will, in turn, help you in-season. When I was an unrestricted free agent, one phone call away from a tryout, I didn't have the luxury of building a foundation.

Now that I was locked in with a team and had six months to get ready, it was time to build, gain and map out a plan to be the fastest, strongest and baddest receiver to enter training camp — and hopefully earn a roster spot. I had a chance, and as an athlete, that's all you can ask for: a chance. As a matter of fact, it doesn't matter if you're an athlete or not, this is a fundamental truth across the board. Are you ready for your chance? Are you ready for your opportunity? Better yet, have you been preparing for an opportunity? Because it is coming, and when it comes, you better be ready! I made sure I was ready for mine.

CHAPTER 18

ROUGHRIDER FOR A SEASON

*"Success is walking from failure to failure
with no loss of enthusiasm."*

– Winston Churchill

As THE PLANE began its descent into Regina, Saskatchewan, it had the familiar look of west Texas: flat with nothing in sight for miles and miles. I don't know what I was expecting, but the flat horizon of fields caught me off guard. Getting through customs was fairly easy. Although I did catch the gentleman working at the immigration desk off guard when he asked me how long I would be visiting Canada and I responded with, "either one week or six months." He pressed further, asking what exactly the purpose of my trip to Canada was. I told him I was there to play football for the Saskatchewan Roughriders and an immediate smile ran across his face from ear to ear, and I instantly knew he was a huge Roughriders fan.

The Saskatchewan Roughriders and the town of Regina reminded me a lot of my time with the Green Bay Packers. In both places, the town comes alive on game day and neither franchise has a traditional owner. They have shareholders and are owned by the citizens, which in turn creates a vested interest in these teams. It creates quite the atmosphere to have fans that carry the title "partial owner" of a professional football team.

The city of Regina is small, compared to what I was used to in Texas. There are two main cities in the province of Saskatchewan. As a newbie in these foreign lands, that's how my new Canadian friends explained the layout to me. There is Regina, a southern city, which is about a two-and-a-half-hour drive from the Montana and North Dakota border. Then there is Saskatoon, which was two hours north of Regina. One thing Saskatoon is famous for is berries. I kept seeing all these TV commercials and billboards advertising how "amazing" these Saskatoon Berries were. I never tried these famous berries, so I can't elaborate on if it was just a lot of hype or if they really are the real deal, but to be honest with you, they looked a whole lot like regular blueberries to me. A few of us found a restaurant called Smokin' Okies which served mouth-watering barbecue! And that means a lot coming from a Texan. The owner was from Oklahoma and prided himself on bringing Southern food up North. We sure were happy he did too!

One of the other receivers the Saskatchewan Roughriders had signed was Eric Morris from Texas Tech. Eric had a phenomenal career at Texas Tech and even had a free-agent tryout with the Chicago Bears. He was hungry for a roster spot just like I was. We played cards and a game I learned in the Green Bay locker room in-between practices and meetings called cribbage. We became instant friends.

As I was fighting for a roster spot on my new team, my brother, Daniel, was just graduating from the University of Arkansas. He was an All-American Long Jumper and Triple Jumper for the Razorbacks. The Arkansas Razorbacks have traditionally been a powerhouse in track and field and cross-country. They have won the most National Championships of any university in his two sports. Daniel was fortunate enough to be part of two National Championships during his career with the Razorbacks and has two fancy rings to prove it. Daniel wasn't sure which direction he wanted to go with his life and career, and knew he needed some time off to relax and think now that his college career had come to an end. I told him that if I made the roster in Saskatchewan, he could come up and spend some time with me in Canada. I only had one rule for him, "You must do the dishes and make your bed every day!" to which he promptly agreed.

The CFL and NFL have a few rule changes that make the game quite different. In the NFL, each team has four downs to move the ball and ten yards for a first down. In the CFL, each team only has three downs: as a wide receiver, this is fantastic news! Since we don't have an extra down like the NFL, by design, most plays are passing plays. Sounds great, right? Well, there is a small catch. The CFL can start with wide receivers behind the line of scrimmage in motion, just like in arena football. That means CFL receivers start roughly ten yards behind the football and get a running start to time it up perfectly for when the ball is snapped. At face value, it seems like the wide receivers have an advantage over the defenders since we get a running start. While it does help to get momentum from going behind the line of scrimmage, it takes a toll on your body. Now every route is ten yards long. For example; a five-yard stop route is when the wide receiver runs five yards from the line of scrimmage and turns around hoping the quarterback has decided to throw the ball to him. A five-yard stop route in the CFL is actually a fifteen-yard route because the wide receiver starts ten-yards behind the line of scrimmage before running the five-yard stop route. Each route run now has an extra ten yards built in due to the running start. That may not sound like a lot, but over the course of a three-hour football game, you must be in extremely good "running" condition to make sure your lungs and legs don't give out on you.

Our first game of the season was against the Edmonton Eskimos, and it was a pretty hot summer afternoon for Canada. The temperature reached into the mid-nineties, and my teammates considered that scorching hot. I laughed and told the guys that the day's weather was a pleasant October day in Texas. I don't think they believed me, but if you live in Texas — or anywhere in the southern part of the United States for that matter — I think you would agree with me.

As I worked to make the roster with an impressive showing versus Edmonton, I wanted to show my versatility by playing on every special teams unit. That included the kick-off team, punt team, kick-off return team and punt return team. I wanted to show my coaches, teammates and the team decision makers that I would be more than willing to help the team win as a wide receiver and special teams player. Three downs in the CFL means there are more special teams plays then in a typical NFL football game. This means there was a lot of running. By a lot, I mean a ton of running with not much resting between offense and special teams.

I made it through our first game and pre-season schedule with a strong response. I played lights out on every play, regardless if I was playing wide receiver or on a special teams unit. I was not going to be denied a roster spot for lack of effort. I can assure you of that.

Once again, it was time for management to trim the roster — a time that every player dreads. No one wants to get the phone call or see the slip in their locker that means it's time to turn in your playbook and head home. Contrary to what you may think, when it comes time to naming the team, there is no big announcement. You simply have a note, or you don't. Feelings from my previous experiences with roster cut day surfaced, and I was uncomfortable and uneasy. I pulled up to the stadium, walked into the football facility and made a beeline straight to my locker. As I surveyed my locker, I didn't see a slip or note to turn in my playbook. Feelings of excitement, joy and relief surfaced and quickly scared away my feelings of discomfort. I thought to myself: *I finally made a team. I'm not going home. It's time to get ready for the football season!* I called my family to share the great news and informed my brother that he had a place to stay in Canada!

The joy of making a team and surviving a cut was incredible. I knew there was plenty of work to be done, but I savored the moment of accomplishing a major goal. In making the final roster, I also made a new friend: Graham Harrell. Graham was an NCAA record-setting quarterback from Texas Tech and had made his way to the CFL after a brief stint with the Cleveland Browns. Graham and I became fast friends and roommates. I mean roommates in the most literal way possible. My brother had stayed in Canada for a month with me for some R&R, and he was about to head back to Texas. I rented a bed for my brother, which we kept in my room, as our living quarters were quite small. When Graham moved in after my brother headed home, we kept the same sleeping arrangements. He would sleep in my room, on the rented bed my brother had used for the last month. I felt like a freshman in college all over again!

There is an interesting rule within the CFL. You can only be at the practice facility and in meetings for a total of four hours per day. It was mandatory from CFL headquarters to release players after four hours of work. After coming from the NFL, I couldn't wrap my mind around this rule, as it was common to spend eight hours a day in the National Football League. This rule allowed us to be out of the facility by 2:00 PM each day, which gave us plenty of time to grab our golf clubs and get to our regularly scheduled tee time of 3:00 PM. Football in the morning, golf in the afternoon; it was a great schedule.

The CFL also has an import to non-import ratio it must follow. This rule simply means that only half of your roster can be American football players, or import, while the other half of the roster has to be Canadian football players, also known as non-import. I believe this rule is in place to keep the CFL tradition alive and continuing to generate interest among Canadian fans to support fellow Canadian football players. The last thing the CFL would want to have happen is to have the league turn into an NFL developmental league where guys come and go like a revolving door. Fans in the Canadian Football League wouldn't have the chance to rally around a star player. I understand the importance of this particular rule and the reason behind implementation, but it did make it even tougher to fight for a roster spot. It was especially hard to see high-performance players get cut in order to satisfy the "import" to "non-import" ratio.

The early part of the season provided a new challenge for me. Although I was on the active roster, I did not have a starting spot. My role was to be a reserve wide receiver and starter on special teams. Due to the fast pace of play in the CFL, reserve wide receivers get ample playing time to help keep everyone fresh. I had to embrace my new role as a backup and complete my job to the very best of my ability, because that was what was best for the team!

We were playing good football and leading our division when our star wide receiver got hurt. He fractured a bone in his ankle, and it was so severe that it put an early end to his season. Everybody knows that injuries are a big part of football. It's simple math, really. The collision of football players hitting each other on every play puts everyone at risk of an injury at any time. In a team sport like football, everybody is supposed to carry a "next one up" mentality. In other words, if one player goes down, another one steps up to make plays so there is no drop off. It's what's best for the team in every situation. This particular injury allowed me to move into a starting position, which would increase my playing time at the wide receiver position drastically.

I had a new pep in my step during practice knowing that I was going to be a starter. I hated to see my friend, teammate and good buddy suffer an injury, but in order to honor him, our teammates and our fans, it was important that I embrace the "next up mentally" and produce at a high level. I played well as a starting wide receiver and caught every ball thrown my way. We were on a nice winning streak, and in my third game as a starter, I scored my first professional football touchdown!

We were on the 29-yard line going in to score, and I was lined up in the outside receiver position. The play called was an all-streak. With an all-streak play, all four receivers run straight down the field as fast as they can. The goal is to put the defense in a tough position where whichever side the safety chooses to go and cover, the quarterback can then safely throw the ball to the other side, away from the safety. As I released off the line of scrimmage with speed, I glanced at the safety and saw him head to the other side of the field. I immediately knew the ball was coming my way. As I looked up towards the quarterback, I saw a perfectly floating football that was going to meet me in the end zone. I continued to track the ball into my hands as a defender who was chasing me tried to close ground and catch up. It was too late for him, as I had already crossed the end zone, scoring my first touchdown. It was unbelievable!

I re-lived the perfect pass all week and was already dreaming of scoring more touchdowns as we made a run in the playoffs. We secured our playoff spot and had one more regular season game that if we won, we would secure home-field advantage throughout the playoffs.

It was a cold rainy night at home versus the Calgary Stampeders. Saskatchewan versus Calgary is a huge rivalry in Canada. It had been a massive rivalry for years, and it always added a bit of gusto to this particular matchup. The score was close going into halftime. We were going to receive the ball at the start of the third quarter, so I began to warm-up my hamstrings as the temperature that night was negative twenty-nine degrees. It was cold, especially when you're a Texas boy. On our sideline, we have these heat jets that everyone huddles around to keep our legs and backsides warm. They are so hot that if you stand too close to it, it will melt your football pants to your leg. I wouldn't recommend trying that at home.

On the first play of the second half, we called a pass play. My route was to run a slant route. When this route is drawn on paper, it looks slanted, hence the name slant route. It's one of the first routes I learned in 7th grade: three steps up, plant and head at a forty-five-degree angle. It's one of the easiest routes to learn and generally one of the first ones taught.

The ball was hiked, and I sprinted up field as fast as I could. One step, two step, three step, time to plant and head at a forty-five angle. When I put my foot in the ground to plant, my foot stayed in the ground while my body went up field. I felt an explosion in my knee and a pain that I had never experienced before in my life. I fell to the ground and immediately grabbed my knee. My mind raced to the worst-case scenario as the pain continued to increase in and around my knee. The officials saw I was down and called an injury timeout while our training staff ran to my side to render aid. I told them what I was feeling, and they hoisted me up to get me into the locker room for a better look at my knee.

I had two of our trainers help me off the field as I put my arms around their neck and used them as human crutches to hobble off the football field. I did not know this at the moment, but that would be my last play as a professional football player. Even as I write these words, all these years later, it still brings out a certain sadness in me. I got into the locker room and collapsed on the training table for our team doctor to assess the situation. The swelling was intense around my knee, so he requested an MRI.

The healthcare system in Canada is very different than the United States. Instead of instant availability for an MRI, which we're accustomed to in the U.S., it took three days to get on the hospital schedule for an MRI. And that is considered lightning fast in Canada. Most people have to wait four to six months for an MRI.

It took twenty-four hours for the MRI to be processed and for the doctor to get the results. As I limped into the hospital, I was hoping that the MRI came back negative and it was just a severe knee sprain. I sat on the patient table as the doctor walked in to give his diagnosis. Sure enough, my worst nightmare was coming true. I blew out my knee. I completely tore my ACL and partially tore my lateral meniscus. Looking back, I think deep down I already knew my knee was in bad shape, but hearing the doctor's report confirm my feeling — after four days of waiting for a proper diagnosis — was heart-wrenching.

I left the hospital and went to the nearest post office. I wanted to get a second opinion, so I mailed my MRI disc to my college doctor. It never hurts to get a second look at things, and I wanted him to provide his own diagnosis of my knee. I built a great rapport with him in college, as he was the one responsible for putting me back together: sort of like I had been Humpty Dumpty. I had three surgeries in college, and he was the lead on all my operations. I came back stronger from each surgery and I truly credit that to his skills of fixing me while I was under the knife. It didn't take long for the disc to reach his office and I received an email with his diagnosis after reading the MRI: torn ACL. It looked like I would be using his services for the fourth time!

We still had a month left in the season if we were to make it all the way through the playoffs and into the Grey Cup. The Grey Cup is the CFL's version of the NFL Super Bowl. This part of the season was tough, especially for American football players, because a majority of us hadn't played in this type of weather. Canadian winters are brutal, and trying to play a three-hour football game outside was a difficult adjustment. Thankfully, we secured home field advantage throughout the playoffs so at least we knew that we would be at home to make a run at the Grey Cup.

I have to admit; it was torture sitting on the bench, walking around on crutches as my teammates went to battle in the playoffs. Everyone knows that injuries are part of football, but when it happens to you, it's an awful feeling. I wanted to do everything in my power to get on the field and help our team win, but my body just wouldn't let me. My knee was a mess and was going to require reconstructive surgery before I could get back on the field to play. There was one small silver lining to this whole situation. By not being able to play in the playoffs, I was able to see how well our team was doing. We were starting to play our best football of the season. Ideally, that's when you want to play your best football — in the playoffs! We played so well that we won our division and secured a spot in the 97th Grey Cup held in Calgary, Alberta.

Calgary is a beautiful place. Every summer the city hosts a stampede that basically shuts down the city. It's like a giant rodeo complete with concerts, exhibitions, shows, cowboys, horses and just about anything country-related that you can think of. The Grey Cup was held the last week in November, so we missed the summer stampede, but we were still able to capture the city's amazing ambiance. We flew in a week before the game, which is pretty standard for a championship game. Each team wants to practice at the host stadium to give players a visual walk-through of what it will be like on game day.

Our team had practice in the morning, reviewing of film in the afternoon and then Grey Cup activities in the evening. The activities typically included a team dinner at a locally-known restaurant, followed by some form of entertainment. I had a brace around my knee to keep the movement at bay, which was especially crucial given all the walking we did in the city. I felt lucky to have the chance to enjoy the week and all the activities the Grey Cup offered, but I still felt like something was missing. The drive, determination and hunger to help my team win on game day were ever present that week. It was super frustrating to sit-in at practice with a brace on my knee knowing that I would play zero downs in the Grey Cup.

I was pretty upset about my predicament. Sometimes I found it easy to blame God when things didn't go the way I thought they should. This time was no different. But what's interesting to see as I get older, is that in the past I would tend not to give credit to God when things went really well — only when things went wrong. I was on an interesting path with my relationship with Jesus. It was essentially on a performance basis. I felt like when I wasn't playing football, or injured, that I had done something wrong and offended God. It felt like I was being punished. Boy was that an exhausting thought process and horrible theology! I know now that there is nothing I can, or can't do, to separate or limit God's love for me. The cool thing is that invitation is a free gift, given on faith alone, which is available to everyone.

Blowing out my knee and sitting in the stands for the Grey Cup game, when I wanted to be out there so badly, put my faith to the test. It was a relatively warm night in Calgary for a football game. The crowd was impressed by the defensive battles and big plays each offense was able to capture periodically. As time ticked down with two minutes to go, we kicked a field goal to take the lead by one point.

Montreal got the ball back and started making a move up the field and into our territory. They were in field goal range with a few seconds left on the clock. My heart started to beat anxiously, and I felt like I was having a nervous breakdown on the sideline. The championship was literally coming down to this final play. Montreal snapped the ball, the kicker approached the ball and kicked it wide of the field goal! WE WON! Everyone on our sideline went wild. I couldn't move much, but I still threw my hands up in the air and celebrated the best I could with my team. Then it happened. About thirty seconds into our celebration, I saw the referees motioning people to get off the field and back on the sideline. There was a lot of confusion as to what exactly was going on. Both teams went back to their sideline and then the head official came over to our head coach and shared some devastating news. There had been a penalty on the final play. We had too many men on the field. This advanced the ball ten yards and the down had to be replayed. We were shocked. We couldn't believe what was going on, and everyone knew there was no way their kicker was going to miss again — especially now that the ball had been moved up ten-yards closer. Montreal snapped the ball, and this time their kicker placed the ball directly through the goalpost uprights and secured the win for Montreal. Their sideline erupted with joy and celebration while our sideline stood in disbelief. We had been Grey Cup champions for thirty seconds. For those thirty seconds, we were on top of the world. Now, we would go down in the Grey Cup history books as a team that came up short. We finally made it to the locker room after sluggishly walking off the field. It was so quiet that you could hear a pin drop in the locker room. Our head coach and other coaches were in the same cloud of sadness we were. Everyone was ready to get the heck out of Calgary and head home to the off-season so we could begin training for the next year and put this game out of memory. I was upset about the game, and also upset about the pay cut. Each player on the winning team won $16,000, and each player on the losing team won $8,000. It was quite the pay cut for such a ghastly loss.

Graham and I had our cars in Saskatchewan for the season and we needed to get them back to Texas. One of Graham's buddies, Brad, flew up for the Grey Cup and then over to Saskatchewan to make the trek home with us to Texas. It would be a twenty-four-hour drive from Regina, Saskatchewan to McKinney, Texas. We got word that a massive snowstorm was about to hit Regina, so we knew we needed to try to get ahead of this thing. We left at 2:30 AM. Not the best time to leave for a long trip, but we didn't have many other options. We didn't want to risk getting stuck in Saskatchewan. We arrived at customs on the border of Saskatchewan and North Dakota at 5:00 AM with our cars fully packed. The border patrol wanted to know where we came from and where we were going. We told them that we were football players for the Saskatchewan Roughriders and were heading home for the off-season. They were big CFL fans and immediately brought up the Grey Cup last-minute field mishap and could feel our pain. Needless to say, they let us clear customs without much trouble.

We drove another couple of hours through North Dakota before stopping at a gas station for breakfast tacos and to top off our gas tanks. As we were leaving the gas station, Graham must have rolled his car through a stop sign as he was immediately pulled over. I saw the flashing lights of the cop car turn on, so I slowed down as he dealt with Graham. It was a long traffic stop, but I did see him write a ticket so I called Graham once he was given permission to leave. I asked what happened and he said he got a ticket. I asked, "Well, how much is it?" He replied, "Probably twenty bucks, but I'm not worried about it." To this day, I'm not sure if Graham ever paid that $20 traffic ticket in North Dakota.

Driving twenty-four-hours is quite the challenge. But we were young, stubborn guys and we were determined to make that drive nonstop. Thankfully we had Brad to join us on this trek giving us the ability to rotate drivers periodically. By hour twenty, I was fighting to keep my eyes open, so we pulled over for Brad to drive my car for a while so I could catch a quick nap.

I finally made it to my parents' home in McKinney at 2:24 AM the next day. Total drive time was twenty-four-hours and four minutes. We drove from Saskatchewan to North Dakota to South Dakota to Nebraska, then to Kansas, Oklahoma and finally Texas — in one sitting. I was so exhausted that I slept for thirteen hours straight, woke up to grab a bite to eat and then went back to bed until the next morning. I don't recommend making that long of a drive, and hopefully will never have to do that again.

Once I gathered my bearings after my Canada to Texas drive, it was time to have surgery. It had been a month since I tore my ACL, so I had been in a brace the entire time. My doctor needed the swelling to go down before he could do the surgery, so the four weeks was perfect to allow the swelling to decrease. I wanted to have my surgery back in Texas instead of in Canada, for obvious reasons. The surgeon I wanted to use was my doctor from the University of North Texas who had done all my surgeries. I liked and trusted him. Plus, each surgery I came back stronger, so it made logical sense.

I had my agent inform the team of my decision, and let's just say they weren't too happy about it. But at this particular time in my life, healthcare in Canada was quite different than healthcare in the United States. Plus, I had an unbelievable facility to rehabilitate my knee after surgery at the Michael Johnson Performance Center. Home is where I wanted to do my surgery and my rehabilitation.

Dr. House scheduled me as his last surgery of the day, so that he could take his time. This was my fourth surgery, so I knew what to expect in terms of prep time. When I saw the anesthesiologist, I knew I was about to be out. I guess it's just my competitive nature, but I always tried so hard to make it to the count of ten. I think my record was only six.

The next thing I remembered was waking up in the hospital and noticing that it was very dark outside. The surgery for my repaired knee should have only taken a couple hours. Instead, it took seven hours! I chose to harvest my hamstring to make my new ACL, but my hamstring was bigger than the doctor had anticipated and the screws he needed for a larger-than-normal hamstring were not available. They had to call medical reps all across the Dallas/Fort Worth Metroplex to bring bigger screws to the surgery room — all while I was knocked out on his table.

Shortly after waking up, Dr. House appeared in my room and echoed what the nurse had also shared. He mentioned that everything looked nice and strong and to be smart during the rehabilitation process. He made sure I understood that I needed to take my time during rehab, and if I followed proper protocol, I would recover thoroughly and my knee would end up even stronger. I liked hearing those words because I had unfinished business that I needed to attend to on the football field.

I received permission from Dr. House to begin rehab the next day. If you have had ACL surgery, or know someone who has, the first step to rehabbing a knee is to get the full range of motion back. I was literally in rehab at the Michael Johnson Performance Center twelve hours after waking up, working on extending my new knee. Full ACL recovery varies for each individual. Sometimes it can take six months, sometimes nine months, and in some cases a full *year* for recovery. I was determined to be on the shorter end of the so-called recovery stick.

I made sure to stay as close to the recovery protocol as possible and would back off on days my knee was killing me. One of the hardest things about my repaired knee was getting back the full range of motion. Lorenzo, my head physical therapist, would take a towel and guide my foot on a flat surface until my knee would bend at a certain angle. He would mark on his chart how much I had improved from week-to-week, and in some cases, it would only be centimeters. On a few occasions I had to bite down on my mouthpiece because it hurt so badly. I even remember crying twice during a few of the range of motion drills.

It took a few months before I was cleared to put full body weight pressure on my knee. Michael Johnson Performance had access to an underwater treadmill that would help alleviate full body weight and allow me to work on my running mechanics underwater. In this tank were also video cameras so my physical therapist could see how my foot was sticking and what the range of motion in my knee looked like. MJP is loaded with top-notch equipment and staff that are some of the best trainers in the world. There's no doubt in my mind that staying plugged in to my training protocol at a facility like MJP helped me speed up my recovery process. I ended up getting medically cleared in five-and-a-half months! I was cleared two weeks before the beginning of training camp. Two weeks before I could be back on the field with my teammates in Saskatchewan, working towards finishing what we started and capturing the ever-elusive Grey Cup title!

With training camp just around the corner, I began to say my good-byes to everyone in Texas. I was so thankful for the staff at MJP for getting me back in playing shape so quickly. It was going to be sad leaving them behind. Then one afternoon my phone rang, and it was an area code from Saskatchewan. At first glance, I thought it might be my receiver coach call-ing to discuss the first few days of training camp and which plays we would install in the offense. I answered the phone, and on the other end was the General Manager of the Saskatchewan Roughriders. After he introduced himself on the phone and got through the pleasantries, he cut to the chase. He told me that they had concerns about my knee, didn't think I would be ready for training camp and were going to have to release me that after-noon. He mentioned that he was going to call my agent after we got off the phone and update him on the roster transaction.

My heart immediately sank, and I didn't know what to say. I don't think I said much. I was in shock that this was happening again. Especially after everything I went through to get my knee back in football shape in only five and half months. I worked so hard! We hung up the phone and tears began to stream down my face. I thought about my conversation with the General Manager at the end of last season when he called me in his office after my injury. He said he believed in me! Well, obviously not enough, because he had just cut me. I didn't know what to do. I was inconsolable.

CHAPTER 19

MY DREAM IS DEAD

"Many of life's failures are people who did not realize how close they were to success when they gave up."

– Thomas A. Edison

I COULD SEE the door closing on my dream as a professional football player. I didn't have any workouts lined up, and the news from my agent was pretty bleak. No one wanted me, plain and simple. Sure, I had become a professional football player at twenty-two years old. My dream had come true! But by age twenty-six, I had been cut three times, lost 2.6 million dollars in NFL contracts and suffered a torn ACL in my right knee. I knew how a football scout would see it: like I was damaged goods.

It felt like my world had come crashing down. Somewhere along the way I had concluded that my value as a person was tied to my achievements as an athlete. If I was a good football player, then I mattered. If I wasn't, I didn't. So, getting cut was more than just getting cut, it was a direct assault on my identity. I needed help understanding that football wasn't the issue, my identity was. It wasn't a football crisis I was having — it was an identity crisis.

I had to lose everything to see that my identity had been tied to worldly successes. Through the process of examining my life, I began to experience a transformation in my heart; I began to feel Jesus calling me back to Him. I started to see that my identity was not based in what I achieved in the world, but rather in what Christ had accomplished on the cross. I need constant reminders of who I am in Christ, what I already possess in Him and how nothing can separate Christ's love for me, no matter how many times I fall short.

Maybe you have been drifting just like I had been for years, and you want to rededicate your life to Christ. Or maybe today is your day to open your heart and ask Jesus to be your Lord and Savior. Feeling connected to Christ's love gave me the confidence to try again with sports.

My competitive bone kept rearing its head as I knew I still had something left in the tank athletically. Wanting to take advantage of the momentum, I signed up to compete in a sprint-triathlon hosted by the Cooper Fitness Center in McKinney, Texas. Dr. Kenneth Cooper started his institute in Dallas and has a fitness center in McKinney as well. My parents had participated in the Cooper Sprint-Tri for a number of years, so my thought process was that if my mom and dad could do it, I certainly could as well. I mean, after all, I was a professional athlete, right?

A sprint triathlon can vary in distance, and for this particular race, it was a 750-meter swim, 12-mile bike ride and 3.1-mile run. I was a bit concerned about the swimming portion since I didn't swim laps regularly, but after seeing it was only seven-and-a-half laps in a pool, I felt better about it. (Boy was I wrong about the swimming! I will get to that in a minute.) I borrowed my dad's 1997 Schwinn bike. It was outdated and a shade of red that really showed its age. I used regular athletic shoes I had been training in for football for the running portion — nothing fancy like I saw many of the other competitors wearing. Many of them even had special running shoes designed specifically for that the race! I felt really out of place when I noticed that.

I think it may have crossed my mind once that I had done zero long distance training, but I quickly plucked it from my memory. I was prepared for a 40-yard dash, since that's what all scouts wanted to see when they brought in football players on a try-out basis. But I wasn't prepared for a 3.1-mile run. Nonetheless, I figured I could just wing it on race day and it would be no problem. Looking back now, this was one of the dumbest decisions I made in my athletic career — thinking that just because I was a professional in one sport, I could make a seamless transition to another without any training whatsoever.

Thankfully it was a cool summer morning in Texas on triathlon day. Conditions were ideal. The first portion of the race was the swim. I waited until it was my turn to jump in the pool. As I dove in, I noticed for a moment how refreshing the water was. I also quickly noticed how fatigued I was from using my limbs to propel myself forward without taking a breath. Roughly halfway through the first lap, I looked up and took a giant gasp. I could see where some of the onlookers may have gotten the impression I was a whale with all the gasping for air I was doing during this swim. I finished the first lap, and instead of doing a cool swimmer's flip-and-turn underneath the water to continue, I stopped, paused and hoisted myself up on the railing to catch my breath. It was then that it finally occurred to me that I was not prepared for this at all — and that I still had 700 meters remaining in the swim.

I took off for the second lap as other friendly competitors kindly passed me in the water. I could have sworn they were all winking at me behind their goggles as a way of poking fun at the rookie triathlon athlete! I was clearly embarrassed at getting passed in the water, but what really added the cherry on top of this humble pie were the words of encouragement from onlookers. Each lap I had to stop, catch my breath and gather my bearings. During these extended breaks on the swimming wall, I started to receive ample amounts of cheering and words of encouragement. I received blessings to keep on pushing forward, or as Dory would say, "Just keep swimming, just keep swimming." You would think having a crowd behind you, chanting and encouraging you, would add fuel to your fire — and normally, it would. In this particular case, however, when I was way out of my league, it added a form of embarrassment to the experience that I hadn't felt in a while.

As I finished my final lap and climbed out of the pool, I knew I needed to put that portion of the race behind me. Years of athletics had taught me that no matter how embarrassing something was, you had to put the past in the past. So by that point in time, I was fairly good at that. What stared me in the face next was the 12-mile bike ride, followed by a 3.1-mile run.

I remember thinking, *how in the world am I going to be able to finish this triathlon? I just spent all of my energy fighting the 750-meter swim!* If you have completed a triathlon before, you know what I'm about to share. If you haven't done a triathlon before, let me fill you in on a potential gear issue. I didn't take into account that I would be sopping wet after the swim and didn't have the proper shorts on for the upcoming ride. 12 miles on a bike is long enough. 12 miles, drenching wet, in the wrong shorts is just plain misery.

The bike ride was uncomfortable, to say the least, but as I saw biker after biker pass me I felt like my 1997 Schwinn was missing a key gear. The gear called SPEED. I didn't have speed and kept getting passed. As I humbly continued to ride, I chalked it up to my equipment. Yeah, my equipment! That's why a 65-year-old grandmother passed me. And in her sweet grandmother voice, she encouraged me to not give up and keep peddling hard. Here's the deal — I am all for encouraging others during a friendly competition — I truly am. But at this point, halfway through my first-ever sprint triathlon, the grandmother who was crushing me on the bike pummeled out any pride I had left that day.

I parked my bike after 12 miles and took off on the run. Did you know that you're not allowed to wear earphones during competition? Well, I had no idea! But apparently it's a safety issue. Anyways, when I run long distances, and by long distance, I mean anything over 400-meters, you better believe I have my earphones on with music blasting to drown out the pain of running long distances. One of the race directors made sure I knew the rules as I took my earphones out and then quietly placed them back in my bag. I was now running 3.1 miles with no music!

Surprisingly I did pretty well on the run. I only had to stop and walk a few times to catch my breath, but I finished! Maybe it had something to do with just wanting to get the miserable triathlon over with, but I finished. And let me tell you, crossing that finish line in whatever place I was in was awesome! Needless to say, my first triathlon performance was embarrassing. But to compete in something I wasn't good at brought a sense of satisfaction. There's something about completing a task that brings a sense of satisfaction for anyone. No matter how well or how poorly you performed, knowing that you finished the task at all is a reward in and of itself.

Maybe you're stuck in an area of your life that you're embarrassed about. Or you're in a place where you feel unqualified and underappreciated. You may even feel like quitting. That's something you could do; there's good wisdom and sense in ending something that doesn't work for you and instead finding something that you're passionate about in an environment in which you are valued. I would encourage you to seek that out in the long term. But in the meantime, I hope that you don't quit what you're working on now. I hope that you see it through and complete the task ahead of you. Remember, you can always recalibrate and recalculate, and that's something we should all do from time to time. But when you're in the thick of things, please know that there will be a sense of satisfaction at the end once your job, task or requirement is complete. You can do it, I promise!

CHAPTER 20

THE ONE

*"You are the finest, loveliest, tenderest, and most beautiful person
I have ever known—and even that is an understatement."*

– F. Scott Fitzgerald

MY ROOMMATE BLAKE and I would spend a few evenings every week at a local golf course. My golf game wasn't much better than my triathlon game, but at least there was no swimming involved. One evening while swinging the links, Blake showed me a picture of his co-worker's best friend who had just graduated from Texas A&M University and moved into the area for work. "Wow, she is HOT," I said out loud, trying to play it cool. I took his phone and started scrolling through her profile pictures on Facebook, which got my heart jumping! Yes, I was creeping hard core.

A couple weeks passed, and thoughts of my dream girl swirled through my mind as I continued to hold onto the small sliver of hope for a new football contract. One evening, Blake invited me to come out and see a local band and mentioned that his co-worker and her friend Amanda, the girl from Texas A&M, would be there. I did what every guy does when he knows he's about to meet his future wife: I put on my Sunday's best! I wore my fedora and Chuck Taylor shoes with shorts and a t-shirt. In other words, I looked like a freaking clown, but a stylish one at that.

Or at least I thought I looked stylish. I found out a year or so later that upon my entrance, Blake had apologized to the group saying, "Sorry, my roommate doesn't normally dress like this. I don't know what his deal is tonight." I didn't know what my deal was either, other than laying eyes on the most beautiful young lady I had ever seen. I didn't get her phone number that evening, but you better believe I sent her a friend request on Facebook. One of the first things I learned about Amanda was that she was a huge fan of Shark Week. I was also a big fan of Shark Week, so we quickly bonded over hammerhead and great white sharks. If you haven't seen Shark Week, be sure to tune in to the Discovery Channel where they spend a week on Shark-related episodes. It's the best!

I wanted to get to know Amanda on a more personal level, so I asked her out, kind of. I asked if she would like to join me in a 5K race that my mom's company was hosting. What a way to ask my future wife out for the first time, huh? I guess I was thinking if I could last through an awful triathlon, surely running a 5K would be a cakewalk. It was indeed a cakewalk, and that turned out to be true for Amanda as well. I called her the night before the race to check-in, make sure she knew what time I was picking her up, the usual. We ended up speaking on the phone for over an hour that night.

I picked Amanda up bright and early on race day, and she walked out to my car with matching shoes and top. I thought wow, this chick really likes the color pink and man, she is so hot! We arrived at the race and I introduced her to my mom and friends who were joining us for the 5K. Amanda had to go to the restroom, so my mom made sure to take her to the employee bathrooms instead of the porta-potties that accompany all races. Only first-class accommodations for my future wife!

The starter for the race called all the participants to the line and shot off the ceremonial gun to begin the race. I took off fast, wanting to get an early lead. I wasn't planning on winning the race, but I was planning on being the first to finish out of the people that I knew, including Amanda! I would glance back periodically and see Amanda. I thought, not only is this chick smoking hot, she is in great shape! As I was approaching the three-mile mark, I took another glance behind me, expecting to see no one I knew. I didn't see anyone I knew except Amanda. She was right in my hip pocket the whole time! I kicked it up a notch to finish first in our group, but she was right behind, crossing the finish line right after me. As I worked to catch my breath after 3.1 miles, we gave each other high fives and I said, "Wow, you are fast!"

My heart was continuing to race the whole way home. Not from the race, but because I wanted to know more about Amanda. I asked if she had plans that evening, which she didn't, so I invited her to the UNT football game. I dropped her off and told her to wear something green if she'd like to cheer for the home team. "I'll pick you up in a few hours," I said. We drove to the University of North Texas, and I explained to her how much I loved my university and told her more about my football career.

CHAPTER 21

DREAM BIG, AGAIN!

"Don't be afraid to go out on a limb. That's where the fruit is."

– H. Jackson Browne

MY WORLD HAD been turned upside down with this new girl in my life. I kept thinking of creative ways to "hang out" with her as I tried to battle what my future would be in my athletic career. In the meantime, I continued to train in the hopes of receiving a phone call from my agent with my next opportunity. I was wiser, I was smarter, and I knew that if I had one more chance, I would make the most out of it. What's funny is that the chance came, but not in the shape of a football. Rather the shape of a 1,300-pound, 85+ MPH bobsled! My mom called from a work conference she was attending where she had met a co-worker who made the Olympic Team in 2010 as a bobsledder. She mentioned my football career and the struggles of getting cut multiple times to this Olympian, and he encouraged her to tell me to give bobsled a try.

I sort of laughed it off at first because the only reference I had for bobsled — and all I could think about — was the movie *Cool Runnings* about the Jamaican bobsled team. Did you know Jamaica had a bobsled team? Jamaica is clearly known for the athletes they produce for the Summer Olympics, such as world-record holders and track stars: Usain Bolt, Asafa Powell and Shelly-Ann Fraser-Pryce. Understandably, this Caribbean country with its warm, tropical climate is not known for Winter sports. But they do have a bobsled team, and they even made a movie about their journey from the small Caribbean island to the 1988 Winter Olympics in Calgary. Spoiler alert: they crashed in curve eight, but the movie is still worth checking out if you haven't already seen it.

I became more and more interested in the sport. But as I learned more about it, I also began to rationalize in my head and tell myself every reason why I wasn't a natural born bobsledder. I thought to myself, "I live in Texas. We do not have snow. I certainly do not have the experience, so why in the world do I think I would be fit to become a bobsledder for the United States of America?"

Shortly after the bobsled seed had been planted in my mind, I received a call from my agent updating me on which football teams would consider bringing me in for a workout. Here is a synopsis of that call: there were none. The door on my football career had officially closed, and although I didn't want to acknowledge it at the time, I knew deep down it was over. Sure, I could have kept going after a football team, attending mini work-outs where you pay an entry fee for some washed-up coach who supposedly coached professionally in the 1970's to evaluate your talent in the hopes that one of his "connections" would land you on a team. But that usually led to nothing. It was a harsh reality, but I knew it was time to move on.

I mentioned bobsled to my agent, and I could hear a jump in his voice. He said: "I actually represented a bobsledder in the 2002 Winter Olympics in Salt Lake City, Utah. He was a driver and his team won the bronze medal." I was both shocked to find this out and impressed all at the same time. My agent went on to share that only two people had played in the NFL and competed in the Winter Olympics. The first person to do it was a guy by the name of Herschel Walker. Herschel made the 1994 U.S. Olympic Team when the Games were hosted in Albertville, France. When I heard that name, and thought of the reputation of a guy like Herschel, I was ready to give it a push: both figuratively and literally! Here is a fun fact for you, Herschel's driver at his Olympics ended up being my head coach at my Olympics. Bobsledding truly is a small world. The second person to play in the NFL and compete in the Winter Olympics is a guy by the name of Jeremy Bloom. He competed in skiing and was quite talented. He even won a handful of world cup medals.

I ended up speaking on the phone to the Olympic bobsledder that my mom met at her work conference. He was very nice and did a great job of giving me a quick run through of what bobsled is and how to get started. Turns out they look for former football players with a track background. You need the strength of a football player to move the heavy object from a standstill at the starting block. You need the speed of a track sprinter to stay with the bobsled once it starts heading down ice and picking up speed. Who knew my background of playing football and running track in college gave me the physical tools to be a successful bobsledder? Anyways, he told me that one of his good friends was an up-and-coming pilot (bobsled driver), and that I should get on the phone with him as an introduction to the sport. I agreed and thought it was a good idea to keep this bobsled ball moving forward.

I continued to train at the Michael Johnson Performance Center to keep in excellent shape, knowing in the back of my mind that I was just one phone call away from my agent and a new opportunity. Since I was in tip-top shape for football, I had one of the coaches film some short-sprinting so I could send it to this pilot for review. I knew you needed to be fast in bobsled to push the sled, so I wanted him to see firsthand the speed I was going to bring to the table.

One of the advantages of social media is that you can meet someone, before you actually meet someone. I did my research on the internet and Facebook to learn as much as I could about this new pilot so that when we got on the phone for the first time, I already had a good idea of what questions to ask. It was a short, but sweet phone conversation, and my interest in bobsled shot up to a new level. I thought to myself, "I want to be a bobsledder!"

The pilot recommended that I meet them in Park City, Utah, in a few months to try out bobsled and see if I liked the sport. I told the pilot, "Okay, I'll come, but I just want to give you a heads up that if my agent finds a football team between now and then, I'm going football!" He acknowledged my statement and said, "I'll see you in a couple months."

My training as a professional athlete began to take a drastic change. I started Googling bobsled and came across an ample amount of YouTube videos of this "bullet machine" slicing through ice to get to the bottom of the track as fast as possible. I couldn't believe my eyes seeing how fast these things were going. I remember thinking *do people really get into the bobsled?* I tried to soak up as much information about bobsled as I could find. As I began to learn more, I realized that becoming a successful bobsledder and making the Olympic Team ultimately came down to two key factors: speed and strength. I needed to be fast and strong. Not one over the other, but both! I needed to be at an elite level to have a chance at becoming an Olympian.

THE RACE OFF

"Endurance is not just the ability to bear a
hard thing, but to turn it into glory."

– William Barclay

THE OLYMPICS HAPPEN every four years. The time in between is an absolute grind while each athlete hopes to secure his or her spot in the Olympic Games. One of the biggest challenges facing U.S. Olympians and Olympic hopefuls is trying to figure out a way to finance the sport. There is little to no funding provided from the United States Olympic Committee (USOC), and athletes have to get very creative in how they support themselves while chasing the Olympic dream. Unfortunately, many athletes rack up an absurd amount of debt in order to pursue their Olympic dreams. Even worse, many hopefuls don't make the Olympic team, so when they leave the sport due to age, or lack of talent, they are carrying this ginormous ball of debt. To be honest, it is quite sad to see as it happened to a few of my teammates. The USOC has been putting programs in place over the years to help educate athletes and provide options for athletes to pursue. It is beginning to move in the right direction, but we are still far away from giving athletes the type of financial support they need in order to train full time and become Olympians.

I knew if I was going to make a run at the Olympic team, I was going to have to figure out a way to pay the bills while I was training, and more importantly while I was traveling out of the country for bobsled season.

Most athletes are presented with two options when it comes to funding: finding sponsors, or working during the off-season. I chose to do both.

I started a company called The Athlete Watch (TAW) (www.theathletewatch.com) to help student-athletes search for scholarships. TAW is a proactive leadership course giving student-athletes tools that they can use in the college recruiting process. Using high-definition cameras, we build sport-specific skills tapes that our student-athletes can send to college coaches. It's such a smooth process for our families that come on board at The Athlete Watch. As a matter of fact, that's why I launched it. My goal was to create a program that would have helped my family during my college recruiting process. We want other athletes' families to be more prepared and more equipped to tackle the college recruiting process.

Starting a business is tough. To start a business that is heavily dependent on digital tools and online programming is even tougher when you don't have a computer or technology background. I needed help getting the idea off the ground. Luckily, I knew who I could call: my good friend Darrel, a former Halo teammate. Darrel was a software engineer for IBM, and he understood what kind of company I was envisioning right away. He listened to what I wanted, helped me brainstorm ways to flesh the idea out and offered to jump in with his IT and programming expertise. I didn't have to sell Darrel much as he almost immediately was on board with what I was looking to do and wanted a piece of this new business. It must have been all the Halo tournaments we played together that reassured him; he knew that he could trust me and he knew that my aggressive instincts often paid off, like when we played Xbox.

As a newly-minted business, we were looking for success stories that would show the world that our program worked. It's not common to have good luck so fast, but our very first student-athlete to join The Athlete Watch knocked it out of the park. He was a sophomore lacrosse player who dreamt of playing in college. I remember his first phone call like it was yesterday — the relief I felt that someone had responded to my idea — and the joy in his voice when he eventually found a scholarship to play at a small school just outside of Chicago. I was so proud of this kid and the work he put in to make his dream come true! We took his success and started reaching out to schools, camps, training facilities, anywhere we could find athletes that wanted to play in college. It has been so rewarding helping student-athletes go after their college dreams. The company's success also provided a much-needed financial boost that helped offset the training and living costs of an Olympic hopeful.

As U.S. Olympians and Olympic hopefuls, we have a non-profit setup for sponsors to make a contribution in exchange for logo placement on our bobsled, on our gear and in our weekly email blasts. We also contract with sponsors to make speaking appearances at their offices during the off-season. Those are just a few examples of the sponsorship trade-offs. Finding corporate and personal sponsors plays a crucial role in an athlete's success. I must say though, telling people that I was a Texas bobsledder aiming for the Winter Olympics sounded a bit like an oxymoron. I received puzzled looks when I told the potential sponsors who I was, what I was looking to accomplish, and that I needed their help on the journey. Once they realized that I was serious and my goal of making the Olympic team wasn't an elaborate joke a colleague was playing on them, we got down to business.

I was very fortunate to find key sponsors — both at the corporate level and personally — to help contribute to my campaign. It did cross my mind a couple of times, especially when I had a bad day of training, how it would feel if I didn't make the Olympic team when all these people were counting on me. I would get anxious thinking about the possibility that I might let them down, but I just had to use my mental training to push myself through those moments and remind myself why I was doing what I was doing.

Have you ever felt the pressure of other peoples' expectations? It can be stressful and frustrating when we let other peoples' expectations determine our self-worth. Instead, I want you to know that your focus, your ability and how you view yourself is what matters.

My wife (fiancée at the time) was working for a graphic design firm that specialized in designing and creating marketing materials for major businesses and Fortune 500 companies. She would bring samples home for me to review and I was always so impressed with the design and quality that her company produced for their clients. One evening we were talking about sponsorships and how I needed to find a way to target more corporate enti- ties, when a thought suddenly occurred to her: what if her company built a marketing piece for me? What if she and her company could create a first-class, professionally-designed bobsled marketing piece to help gener- ate sponsorships leading up to the Olympics? I was thrilled with her idea and with the fact that my fiancée and I would be working together on this project, tackling what had seemed like an insurmountable obstacle only a few weeks prior.

Amanda set up a conference call with her CEO and a designer to talk through logistics and a timeline. It was encouraging to hear how excited everyone was about designing my bobsled marketing piece. Her company was kind enough to donate the design work as a form of sponsorship, which I was sincerely grateful for. I remember taking a look at the finished piece, inside its glossy cover, and being struck by how professional and appealing it was — it looked amazing! My new marketing materials gave me a real shot at getting corporations to take the Texas bobsledder seriously when it came to pursuing the Winter Olympics.

During the four-year grind of starting a business and raising sponsor- ship money, Team USA Bobsled had a competition season each year. We would start off each season with a combine where each athlete was put through individual testing to see how fast, strong and in shape they were. The weight room portion of our combine consisted of a one-repetition maximum on power clean and a three-repetition maximum on squat. For the outdoor section of the combine, we were taken to a track to run a 60-meter dash. We used fully automatic timing devices for the times and splits of each athlete. Although we were only running a 60-meter dash, we had timers setup at 15-meters, 30-meters and 45-meters. We would receive four timing splits after the completion of each 60-meter dash. We would also be tested on a standing broad jump into a sand pit and then a shot toss throw using both hands, throwing granny style.

As a bobsled push athlete, it is imperative to test well at the combine each year. It's the first ranking each athlete receives and is essential cri- teria the coaching staff uses when evaluating and selecting the National Team. After the combine, we have push championships where each athlete is required to push the bobsled from the back of the sled (brakes) and from the side of the sled (right or left — each athlete chooses his or her particular side.) While you want to test well in the combine, it is even more important that you perform well during push championships. This is the only time athletes will push the bobsled by themselves, giving the coaching staff a unique way to evaluate how well an athlete can do on his or her own. It is very hard to make the team if you do not push well during push championships.

Just like in any sport, I knew that in order to have success in-season you had to take care of business out of season. I would show up to the combine and push championships well prepared from my off-season lifting and sprinting program. I always finished towards the top in both the combine and push championships each season, setting a strong precedent to be named to the U.S. National Team.

We always had two teams on the U.S. National Bobsled team, and some seasons we even qualified three teams. The year that you want to have three teams is Olympic year so more guys have a chance to make the Olympic team. How well each team places during world cup races determines the number of qualifying teams. Our USA-1 crew was solid. They won Gold in the 4-man competition in the 2010 Winter Olympics in Vancouver, Canada. Their team was set on push athletes, and they would continue to dominate the world cup circuit throughout the four-year journey to the 2014 Winter Olympics in Sochi, Russia.

I found myself bouncing back and forth between USA-2 and USA-3. In a sport where everything comes down to a 100th of a second, anytime someone switches teams, there can be a lack of chemistry that directly affects the end result. To ensure a spot on the Olympic team, I needed to be a consistent contender on the USA-2 sled, working towards a race-off with some of the USA-1 guys. A race-off is when two push athletes are compared against each other. One athlete takes the first push, while the second athlete waits for his turn to push. There are a lot of factors that play into the race-off scenario, and it's an art as to who goes first or second for the race-off. I always preferred going first, but some guys like to see what time they need to beat and therefore would rather watch the other guy and then go second.

I had quite a few race-offs during my time in bobsled, but there was one that stands out in particular. It was the year before the Olympics, my third year in the sport, and I was set to race-off against a 2010 Olympian. He was an incredible athlete, and we were both fighting for a position on the USA-2, four-man bobsled. I won the coin toss, so I selected to go first in the race-off. Obviously, I took race-offs very seriously, but I also took practice pushes just as seriously. I learned early on in professional sports that even practice reps matter in terms of future coaching decisions. I have always been a full-speed, all-out practice player, even during my football days. It must have been ingrained in my head from a young age that how you practice will determine how you play. I always wanted to play at a highly-productive level, so I knew that I needed to practice at the same level of intensity.

I warmed up for my race-off like I did on a traditional race day and blasted the sled off the starting block. I felt strong and powerful behind the block. I wanted to crush the bobsled and then pick up sprinting speed to accelerate it as fast as possible. Each bobsled track is roughly a mile long. Our race-off was on our home course in Lake Placid, NY, a course that all U.S. athletes know very well. As I sat in the bobsled heading down the mile track at 80 miles an hour I wondered, *did I push fast enough to win?* We crossed the finish line and saw that we had pushed 5.10 seconds at the start. This was a strong start, and I felt really good about my chances of winning the race-off. Anything under 5.15 seconds in practice is very good.

As we made our way back to the top of the track and loaded our bob-sled for the second run, a few of my teammates, including my buddy who I was racing off, came over to tell me that they were impressed with my push time. It felt good to hear their compliments, but I knew it didn't mean anything unless my time proved to be the fastest time.

My buddy lined up for his push and they blasted the sled off the line. He also looked strong, powerful and fast. As they loaded into the sled, I anxiously watched the starting clock and saw a time of 5.13 seconds pop-up on the screen. I had won the race-off by .03 seconds! I was in shock that

I had beaten an Olympian from 2010 and secured my spot on the USA-2 team; or at least I thought I had. My teammates came over and congratulated me on the race-off win and I had a giant smile from ear to ear as we walked into the bobsled garage to store our sleds after practice. My buddy who I was racing off is a wonderful guy, he came up to me and told me, "Good job," and we shook hands. I had a lot of respect for him, and still do to this day.

I started to gather my gear to head back to the Olympic Training Center when my head coach asked to speak to me. The tone of his voice let me know that we were going to discuss something very important. He too congratulated me on my race-off win, but then went on to say that he wasn't going to make a change. In other words, he was essentially saying, *I know you won the race-off, but there are some "other factors" I take into consideration; therefore, there will not be a change.* As I heard the words echo off his lips, I couldn't believe what was happening. I politely asked him to elaborate in more detail as to why. Since I won the race-off, why wouldn't I take my teammate's spot? I never got a clear answer. He continued to talk in circles and mention these "other factors." I didn't even begin to understand his rationale, maybe because I was so livid about what was happening. I won, yet I lost. That was a tough equation to follow.

I remember the drive back to the Olympic Training Center, feeling like I was sitting under a cloud of utter disappointment and confusion. A couple of veterans in the sport patted me on the back and began to reason with me. They too were confused by our head coach's choice not to honor the race-off win. They also mentioned that this wasn't the first time this kind of thing had happened. In the past, the coaching staff had made "executive decisions" regardless of how a race-off played out. Initially, a sense of relief poked through the clouds when I heard that I wasn't the first guy to go through this experience, but then a sense of astonishment raced through my mind thinking of the other guys who had been in this same position of having a race-off go void. You can imagine the frustration that set in as I kept replaying the conversation in the bobsled garage with my head coach. I won the race-off fair and square, yet he made a decision not to honor the race-off results and keep the roster as it was.

This was the first time in my athletic career where I felt like I was truly robbed. I had constantly been doubted on my athletic ability throughout my life, and that had instilled in me a tremendous drive to produce at a high level. I had no problem out-working the competition; what I did have a problem with was doing things the right way, winning a race-off fair and square and then for "some reason" not being awarded the spot that was up for grabs, that I had essentially earned. I sat in my room at the Olympic Training Center in shock. I was confused and didn't know how to move forward. How do I move up the roster if winning a heads up race-off is not enough and the makeup of the teams is ultimately up to the coach's discretion? The reality of this left a sour taste in my mouth and a giant load of bitterness in my heart.

As with anything in life, we always have options. Even when things get tough and aren't working out the way we anticipate, we always have a couple of options. Part of me wanted to pack it up and head home. I had been robbed of something I earned. It had been blatantly taken away from me. I didn't understand why. It was not fair. I do want to note, if I had chosen to go home and leave the program, I would have been justified about having been treated unfairly; it was 100% unfair that I won the race-off but was not promoted. Had I left at that point, all of my family and friends back home would have clearly understood why I left the program. As a matter of fact, they would have echoed the same response I had on how unfair, unjust and poorly I was treated by my head coach.

I also had the option to stay and to continue to go after my dream, regardless of what had happened. I knew what the right decision was, but it was still hard to choose under those circumstances. I knew if I was going to stay and pursue my dream of making the United States Olympic team, I would have to compete at a level so high that the coaching staff would have no earthly choice but to put me on the Olympic team. As a Christ follower, I would continue to remind myself that how I handled these tough times had a direct correlation with my trust in God and his perfect plan for my life.

Although I was still upset about the race-off, I was relieved that I was at least able to secure a spot on the U.S. National Team as a member of the USA-3 sled. The good news was that as a member of the U.S. National Team, I would travel and compete on the World Cup circuit. The bad news was that the USA-3 sled was typically a revolving door. That meant that our coaching staff would move guys around and try new guys on USA-3 to see how they did. In other words, the USA-1 and USA-2 sleds were the ones you wanted to be on, while the USA-3 sled was up in the air from week-to-week. You never knew who would be pushing that sled. I hoped and prayed it would be me.

CHAPTER 23

COLD, BROKE AND
UP ALL NIGHT

ONE OF THE perks of being on the U.S. National Team was traveling and competing in different locations in North America and Europe. I have competed in Austria, Canada, France, Germany, Italy, Russia and Switzerland. My favorite track in the world is in St. Moritz, Switzerland. St. Moritz is this beautiful town, located in the heart of the Swiss Alps. The food at our hotel in Switzerland was amazing. I particularly enjoyed the dessert bar as I have quite the sweet tooth. St. Moritz is the only track in the world that is made up of all natural ice. Each year a crew literally cuts ice to form the bobsled track. Therefore, each year, the curves on the track and the start ramp are always a little bit different. They have one area of the track called "Horseshoe" where the staff brings in extra metal backing to strengthen the curve. Once you hit "Horseshoe," it propels your sled straight down, pulling four to give g-forces. It is an awesome but scary curve!

Another favorite bobsled location of mine was La Plagne, France. I was always excited to see that quaint town, located in the French Alps, on our bobsled schedule. In order to get to La Plagne, each vehicle had to make over twenty-five hairpin turns. It was especially scary at nighttime, but the view in the morning when the sun came up over the Alps was unbelievable. At sunset in La Plagne, I would FaceTime Amanda to show her that the hotel was above the clouds and the sun was parting over the French Alps. I don't think she appreciated the view as much as I did, mostly because she was sitting in bumper-to-bumper traffic on the Dallas North Tollway.

Once we are in season and on the European circuit, we stay in each location for a week. Monday is a rest day, or sometimes can be an extra practice day. Tuesday, Wednesday and Thursday are practice days. Friday is for rest and to prepare the bobsled for competition day. Saturday is the two-man bobsled race, and Sunday is the four-man bobsled race. Once the four-man race is over on Sunday, everyone hits the road. Each country packs up their vans with bobsleds, weights, luggage and everything else and books it to the next location. It's fairly common to see other countries on the road together and just like in bobsled, we are all racing to the next location.

BMW was a big sponsor of ours and would supply us with X5s and X6s. There's no doubt we had a leg up in the competition getting from one location to another. We would all take turns driving the BMW's, and when we were in Germany, we would put the pedal to the metal on the autobahn. The X5 drove so smoothly. In fact, it was so smooth that I got pulled over in Austria. The police cars in Austria are a bit different than a traditional police car in the United States. An SUV pulled up next to me on the highway. We were both going well over 100 MPH. I looked out the driver side window and saw a single blue light rotating like a police light and a passenger in the car mouthing "pull over." I slowed down and looked for a place to pull over.

I must have missed the sign that said "Leaving Germany, Entering Austria", because we were no longer in Germany. As the police officer walked to our car, I was replaying in my mind how impressed I was that his SUV had been able to keep up with the X5 I was driving. He asked if I knew how fast I was going, which I did not. I mentioned that I thought we were still on the German Autobahn and he clued me in that the Autobahn ended 5 kilometers (2.2 miles) ago and that I was on Austrian roads that have a speed limit. He looked into the back seat of the X5 to see who I was transporting and asked where we were going. I told him we were on the U.S. Bobsled team and heading to Igls, Austria for our next race. It turns out that the officer and his partner were huge bobsled fans. I could see the serious look on his face turn into a soft smile. He asked how the season was going for us and wanted to know where everyone sat in the bobsled. For a moment, I thought I was going to get lucky and get off with a warning and be on my way. He went back to his vehicle to check something and then asked me to get out of the car.

He motioned me over to his car. Confused, I walked hesitantly over to his truck and saw a payment reader. If you have a traffic violation in the United States, the officer gives you a ticket and then you are supposed to call the courthouse in the particular county you received the ticket and either settle up, or fight it. In Austria, they do things a little differently — you pay for your speeding ticket on the spot. The officer's English was pretty good, so I asked him how much the ticket was for. He told me 400 Euros ($600 USD at the time). I was in shock as there was no way my speeding ticket should be $600. I politely told the officer that I couldn't pay that amount. I didn't have that kind of money on me, and besides, how fast was I going? The officer went to the front of the police car to talk to his partner briefly and then came back to visit with me. He told me, "Okay, it's going to be 78 Euro. Please pay 78 Euro." I was thrown off by the randomness of the number, but nonetheless immediately pulled out my wallet to settle up, as this was a much more manageable number.

I had a team credit card that I could use to pay for the speeding ticket; our coaching staff gives each team a credit card for gas and any other car-related expenses that might come up while traveling. I thought to myself, this ticket is 100% car-related, so I gave the officer the Team USA credit card I had in my wallet to pay the fine. As the officer swiped the card for payment, I was already preparing a story in my mind for when my coach would ask me what the 78 Euro charge from the Austrian police was for. I could see the officer was having trouble with the card, so I asked him if everything was okay. He said that the credit card didn't work and that he would need another form of payment. Who knows, maybe Team USA puts a block on credit cards for speeding tickets? Maybe I wasn't the first athlete to think on my feet and try to bill a ticket to Team USA. I gave the officer my credit card, and the payment went through. He handed me a receipt to sign and then gave me a copy. I didn't receive an official speeding citation, just a receipt for 78 Euro.

As you can imagine, spending four years on the road with Team USA, with half the time in Europe, led to many memorable stories involving my teammates. The Austrian speeding ticket was quite the experience on the bobsled tour, but nothing compared to the mistake I made traveling from Winterberg, Germany to La Plagne, France.

It was a Sunday in January, and we had just finished the four-man race in Winterberg, Germany. The weather was nasty. Of course, it always seemed to be bad weather when we competed in Winterberg. Everyone was racing back to our hotel, Winterberg Resort, to pack and hit the road for La Plagne. The word "resort" was a little bit deceptive in terms of this particular hotel. When I think of a resort, I think of five-star accommodations. I can assure you that this hotel was not that. Anyways, back to the drive ahead of us. This drive on a regular day takes nine hours. Everyone on the bobsled circuit was a little upset when they released the schedule because this was by far the longest drive of the season. Typically, the powers that be schedule the season so no drive is longer than four to five hours. For whatever reason, these two cities were next to each other on the calendar, so we had a long drive to make after the four-man bobsled race.

This wasn't a regular day in Europe. It was mid-January, and the snow was coming down hard. Our nine-hour drive would be an eleven-hour drive due to the weather conditions. When we travel, each team has two vehicles. One vehicle is our BMW and the other vehicle is a Sprinter Van. The Sprinter is long enough to hold two bobsleds along with bags, weights, medical equipment and anything else Team USA travels with on the road. The goal is to pack the Sprinter Van as heavily as possible so we have more room in the BMW. I was scheduled to ride in the BMW for this trip, which I was happy about. I still needed to get the keys to the Sprinter Van to throw in my last bag. I grabbed the keys from my teammate and headed out to the van. The van was packed pretty tightly, but I was able to find a spot for my luggage. Somehow between the time when I loaded my bag into the Sprinter Van and the time when I jumped into the BMW to hit the road, I got distracted and forgot to give back the keys to the van. And to make matters even worse, no one in our BMW had elected to upgrade his phone to the European cell service, so for the eleven-hour drive to La Plagne, France, I had no idea that the keys were in my pocket.

We arrived in La Plagne at 2:30 AM and were all exhausted from the drive. I grabbed my backpack and was the first one from my team to walk into the lobby. One of the bobsled drivers was charging his laptop when he looked up and said, "Johnny, you never gave the keys back for the Sprinter Van. It's still in Winterberg." I was baffled by his statement and tried to process what he had just said. I reached into my jacket thinking there was no way I had forgotten to give those keys back, and I immediately felt the cold grip of the keychain. My heart instantly sank. I pulled the keys out and dangled them in front me in complete disbelief. My heart was racing and I felt total anxiety about the crucial mistake I had made. I woke my coaching staff up and told them that I had the keys and that I was so sorry for what had happened. I told them I would head back to Winterberg tonight to get the van, but that I needed someone to ride with me because they would have to drive the BMW back, while I drove the van back.

My coach was pleased to know that we had found the keys. They were in the process of reaching out to the rental car company and having them make a new set of keys as they thought the keys had been lost. There was no question I was ready to make wrong right by heading back to Germany, but my coach recommended that I get some sleep and head back in the morning. As much as I wanted to fix my mistake immediately, it was the right call to get some sleep first, because I had some serious driving to do to get back to Germany and then back to La Plagne the following morning.

As I lay in bed that night, it took me forever to fall asleep. My heart was pumping, and I couldn't believe I had made such a silly mistake. This mistake was going to impact the entire team. Locked in the van in Winterberg were two bobsleds, luggage for most of my teammates and our weight room set. My mistake was going to alter all of our training schedules because now there were no weights available for training on Monday. Many of my teammates were stuck in the clothes they traveled in because their suitcases were in the locked van. I kept replaying in my mind over and over who was going to be impacted by my mistake and I kept arriving at the same conclusion: it was everyone. Everyone on Team USA would have to adjust their plans because of my mistake. I don't know how I slept that night, but I was able to get a few hours of shuteye before the sun rose.

I am pretty sure my teammates hated me, but at breakfast the next morning they showed me some empathy. Everyone knew my mistake was an accident and could see how horrible I felt just by looking at me — it was written all over my face. I ate quickly because time was ticking. I needed to get on the road, but I also knew I needed to break the news to our rookie bobsledder that he would be joining me on my long trek through Europe. His name was Nic, and he was the only rookie traveling with us so there was no need to draw straws or flip a coin to see who would be my riding partner. I told Nic I needed his help and he had a big smile on his face. He really was a good sport and was ready to go right away. I thought to myself, *I wish I was this happy right now, but we have to hit the road if we are going to make it back by tomorrow.*

Once we got on the road, I felt relief because I knew we were that much closer to picking the van up in Germany and getting back to France. The weather was nice in France, but the roads in Switzerland started to get a little hairy. Once we entered Germany, we drove through a snowstorm and finally pulled up to Winterberg Resort eleven hours later. The van was covered in snow, so Nic and I started to dig around the tires in order to put chains on the wheels. I hopped in the van to crank up the heat, but to no avail: the van wouldn't start. I tried again, this time more persistently turning the key, but still nothing. The problem was clear; the van would not start. The lights in the van wouldn't turn on either, which led me to the quick diagnosis that we had a dead battery. I marched into the resort and went straight to the front desk. The desk attendant was surprised to see me as all the bobsledders had checked out yesterday. I filled her in on what happened, and she could feel my pain. I asked her if someone could jump my battery and she ran and grabbed the chef. He said it would be a minute as he was preparing meals for the guests. I decided not to push my luck by asking if anyone else could jump my van besides the chef. Instead, Nic and I patiently waited in the lobby for the chef. Come to think of it, it's sort of hilarious that the chef was the only one who could jump the van. It seems random. Why was he the only person with automotive skills?

Neither one of us had a European cell phone plan, so we grabbed our laptops to kill time and logged on to the internet. Once I was connected, I called my fiancée, who had been briefed the entire time about my mishap. I let her know that phase one of rectifying my mistake was complete. We had arrived in Winterberg and were waiting on the chef and his jumper cables. I also called the coaching staff to let them know the progress of my mission. My social media accounts were blowing up with responses from other bobsledders who heard what happened and felt my pain. I even received an email from Canada-1's driver asking if I could bring his pillow. No, that wasn't a joke. He had forgotten his pillow, and since he heard that I was heading back to Winterberg Resort, he asked if I could kindly grab his pillow. I obliged and retrieved his pillow for him.

Dinner was finally over, and the chef helped jump the van, and we were on our way back to La Plagne. Nic and I were exhausted from two days of driving across Europe, so we decided to only drive a couple hours that night. We pulled into Munich, Germany around 1:00 AM and found a hotel to lay our heads down for the night. I woke up early again and nudged Nic, letting him know that it was time to go. We grabbed a quick breakfast and hit the road. I was counting the hours to La Plagne, and the math said we could make it back in time for practice. I wanted to get my teammates their luggage, the drivers their bobsleds and everyone needed to lift weights! Starting the drive in Munich, Germany, instead of Winterberg, meant we only had a nine-hour drive this time. We put the pedal to the metal and cruised into La Plagne 90 minutes before practice. Everyone was happy to see us because they knew when they saw me, it meant they were about to get all their gear back.

As everyone was unloading their bags, I found out that one of my teammates was nursing an injury from the previous day's practice. With him out of commission, I was next up to fill his spot. After driving 33 hours over the course of three days, my legs were toast. They felt like cinder blocks from sitting stationary all that time. As much as I wanted to rest my legs after driving across Europe, that option wasn't available. Warming up that afternoon was brutal, and although I went full speed in practice, I made sure to keep a close watch on my hamstrings. The last thing I needed was an injury to top off my three-day driving escapade.

La Plagne is one of my favorite bobsled tracks. The track is fun, the hotel is great and the food is excellent. Unfortunately for me, the early part of this trip to La Plagne was spent on the road going back and forth from Germany. I was so thankful to get everybody their gear and be back on schedule with Team USA. Three days and 33 hours later, I could finally sleep in peace. I told myself that I would never let a mistake like that happen again. My teammates also made sure that mistake never happened again; on every future trip, right before we'd leave town, somebody would search my pockets and make sure I didn't have the keys. It was a precautionary measure, but one that guaranteed I'd never leave another van behind.

CHAPTER 24

THE ULTIMATE TEST

"While your circumstances are beyond your control, your character is not."

– John Maxwell

THERE IS A myth that floats around the Olympic Training Center. I'm not sure if it's a myth for all of Team USA sports, but it was ever rampant in bobsled. The myth was that if you didn't live in the Olympic Training Center, then you would not make the Olympic team. As a rookie bobsledder, I sat in a meeting to help introduce new bobsledders to the sport. I was caught off guard by this myth at first and didn't pay it much attention, but it kept coming up over the years leading up to the Olympics. It would go something like this: "If you want to put yourself in the best possible position to make the Olympic team, then you need to live and train at the Olympic Training Center." I was always under the impression that if you produced at a high level, consistently over time, you earned your spot on the team. Whether it was for the Olympics, football or any sport, I thought that was how it worked as an athlete.

Going into the Olympic year, the stakes were increasingly high. Not only was I trying to secure a spot on the Olympic team, but I was trying to make the Olympic team as a non-resident athlete; as someone who didn't live in the Olympic Training Center. In order to live in the off-season and during in-season as well, it was imperative that I worked and raise sponsorship money to offset the costs of becoming an Olympian. Amanda and I were continuing to get serious in our relationship and had started to dream about spending forever together. I needed to pay the bills and invest in my relationship with my future wife. Oh, and make the Olympic team.

I was so thankful for the Michael Johnson Performance Center (MJP), which was located ten minutes from my house. To have a first-class performance training facility in my backyard was unbelievable! The myth of not living in the Olympic Training Center continued to grow stronger as we got closer to the Olympics and I kept telling my teammates and coaches that MJP was as good, and in my personal opinion, more advanced than the Olympic Training Center. I actually felt like I was getting a leg up on the competition living at home and training at a world-class facility.

The power of technology even allowed me to keep in touch with my strength and conditioning coach, Dr. Brad DeWeese. I met Dr. DeWeese at the Olympic Training Center, and after doing my due diligence, realized how knowledgeable this man was in performance training. He began writing my weight lifting and sprinting program — and I followed his programing to a tee. Dr. DeWeese would send me the workout plan for two or three weeks at a time. In turn, I would record my workouts, capture them on video and upload the videos to the cloud for him to review. He coached me remotely for a couple of years, and it worked flawlessly. Although I wasn't living at the Olympic Training Center, I still visited once a month to push a bobsled and stay acclimated to pushing. During the summer months, we pushed a bobsled on wheels. I know that sounds strange, but it's actually the closest that you can get to pushing a bobsled on ice.

Each month when I would visit the Olympic Training Center for push practice, I would also report to the weight room for Dr. DeWeese's testing program. He would measure my body fat, the circumference of muscle groups and conduct other highly sophisticated tests to track my progress. Heading into the Olympic year he had three years of data on me, which gave him ample benchmarking on what exactly I needed to do to produce at a high level. Every time I reported to the Olympic Training Center, I would get immediate feedback on whether the previous month's training program had gone well, or if we needed to adjust the programming. Things were really starting to line up. I felt like I had the non-resident myth under control because my testing numbers were top of the class. Little did I know I was about to have a rude awakening.

As I began preparing for the Olympic Trials, I found out that Dr. DeWeese was leaving the Olympic Training Center for a new position at a university in Tennessee. It was an excellent opportunity for him and his family, so the move made sense. Where it didn't make sense on my end was battling the non-resident myth. Not only was I training from home, my strength coach was now training me from a new location and wasn't at the Olympic Training Center. Honestly, I didn't think it was that big of a deal. I thought to myself, *so what, my workouts are sent to me remotely from an IP address in Tennessee now? I'm still putting in the work, and I will still produce at a high level. Isn't that the point of professional athletics? Whoever produces at the highest marks and level earns the spot?* But you know how myths go — they get blown out of proportion, and sometimes the "myth gasoline" gets thrown on the "myth fire" — and things begin to heat up quickly!

In order to cool the "myth flame," it was imperative that I reported to Olympic testing in the best shape of my entire life. I had been eyeing some of the record board numbers in the weight room, especially the power clean. The power clean is an explosive, lower body lift where you essentially pick the weight off the ground and forcefully lift it to your shoulders. Olympic Trials on ice would begin in October, but in July we were ordered to report to Calgary, Canada for the combine and push championships for Olympic Testing. Calgary Olympic Park is a very nice area. They held the Olympics there in 1988, where the Jamaican bobsled team made their debut and where their movie *Cool Runnings* took place. Calgary also has an ice house that they keep cold year round. With this being the Olympic year, the coaching staff wanted to see everyone's push numbers on ice for more accurate and proper evaluation. I made an effort to take a trip by myself to Calgary to get some push time on ice prior to the testing in July. It was important for me to take mental reps as well as actual reps on the surface for which my Olympic portfolio would be graded upon.

I spent a few days in the Calgary ice house, and on the last day, I had a visitor. His name was Steve Mesler, and he was part of the U.S. Olympic Bobsled Team in 2010 when their four-man crew won the Gold Medal.

It was the first Gold for U.S. Bobsled in 62 years. Mesler's name would come up during my four-year journey from some of my other teammates and coaches; they would talk about how technically sound of a push athlete he was and about the knowledge he had amassed in the sport. Mesler offered to coach my practice pushes and provide feedback on what I could do better off the start block in order to push the sled faster. I ate up everything this Olympic Champion was coaching me on. I made sure that every word that he shared during practice was etched into my memory for later use. I knew that I needed all the advice I could get, as it would ultimately come down to hundredths of a second in making the Olympic team.

The trip to Calgary was the right call athletically in preparation for the biggest test of my life. I also brought Amanda with me on this trip, and we spent a few days after my push practice in Banff Lake Louise, Canada, which is about two and half hours west of Calgary. Let me tell you something about Canada if you haven't been in the summer time: it is absolutely gorgeous. We stayed at the Fairmont Chateau Lake Louise in Banff. We hiked trails, kayaked and even saw a couple of grizzly bears. It was a wonderful time and a much needed mental break before the start of the season.

As July approached, I began to taper off on my training program. All that meant is that I backed off on the weights and sprints in order to let my body recover; this way I would be in an optimal position to perform. I was ready for our first test: the combine. I had been testing my numbers over the course of the summer at the Michael Johnson Performance Center, and I was putting up some strong numbers. Now it was time to showcase all my hard work and ability so that I could make the team.

We started on the track for the 60-meter dash. When we ran the 60-meter dash, we had laser markers at the 15-meter mark, 30-meter mark and 45-meter mark. By running one 60-meter dash, it would spit out four numbers on the computer screen in which we would be ranked. As I stepped to the starting line, I knew it was time to lay it all on the line. I took a deep breath and went to work. I exploded off the line faster than I ever have in my entire life and cruised down the track at optimal speed. I made sure to run through 65 meters so there was no error of letting up too early. As I slowed down to catch my breath and walk back to the coaching staff to see my sprint numbers, I felt really good about my performance. It was time to see what the timer said, and hopefully, it would confirm my positive feelings. I took a look at the chart and an immense feeling of joy set in. In all four measurements, I scored the highest possible cap — 100 points at each mark. Therefore, my total sprint score was 400 out of 400 points. I had aced the sprint test! I was so fired up to see those numbers; it turned out that I had run the second fastest 60-meter dash on the U.S. Bobsled Team!

The momentum from the sprints carried into the remainder of the combine testing. I crushed the weight room tests. Those tests consisted of one power clean at 330 pounds and three squat repetitions at 440 pounds. Both of those marks needed to be hit in order to score 200 out of 200 points. I struggled a little bit in the broad jump, scoring 89 out of 100, but I finished strong in the shot put toss with 98 out of 100. My total score was 787/800 points. This put me in second place overall in the combine testing.

I had always tested well over the years in the combine, but this was by far my highest placement, finishing second overall. The timing to score my best combine finish couldn't have been better! I was extremely pleased with how well I did at the combine, but the focus immediately turned to push championships, which would be taking place two days later. I sat in the ice tub at the Calgary Olympic Park, post-combine, to begin the recovery process on my legs and boy was it cold! Something about ice in Canada, even in July, is still so cold. I knew I needed a big push during push championships to make my mark.

The night before push championships, our coaching staff held a team meeting so we could learn our order for the competition. Since I finished second overall in the combine, I was the second person to select my start number. Some guys think going later is better: their rationale is that going later means you can see everyone else's push times up until your start. Instead, I chose to select position number one. My rationale was that instead of waiting around to see what other guys were pushing, I would set the tone and be the first one to kick off the competition!

My legs felt pretty good as I warmed up and my thoughts went to blasting the sled off the start block. I kept going through the mental checklist that Steve Mesler had given me a few weeks prior. My first push felt strong, and it was fast! Everyone was required to push from behind the bobsled with the first push and then the second push was from the side. My entire career as a bobsledder, I had either pushed from behind the sled (in a position called the brakeman) or from the right side of the sled (in a position called a side pusher). We had a strong roster of athletes who could push from the back of the sled, and as much as I wanted to be a brakeman, I knew my opportunity was from the right side. After the first round had come to completion, I was sitting tied for 5th with a brake push of 5.11 seconds. The start record at Calgary had been broken during the first round by one of my teammates, 2010 Olympian Chris Fogt. He pushed a blazing fast time of 4.96 seconds. Second place came through at 5.00 seconds from Steve Langton, who was Chris' teammate at the Olympics in 2010. Third place after round one was a 5.09-second push from Curt Tomasevicz, who was working on his third Olympic games after winning gold in 2010 in the four-man bobsled. Fourth place was a 5.10-second push, and there I was tied with another teammate in 5th place with a 5.11-second push.

I dialed in my technique on the right side push and laid it on the line again. As I pushed the sled down the Calgary Ice House, I tried to apply as much power and speed to the sled as physically possible. This race was going to come down to hundredths of seconds and I needed to be on top. My right side push came in at 5.12 seconds, which happened to be the 2nd fastest side push of the competition. Steve Langton registered the fastest side push with a smoking hot time of 5.00 seconds.

Everyone had the option to push a third time. If you chose to do so, you were allowed to choose whether you would redo your side push or back of the sled push. Only the best scores count towards your overall ranking. Many athletes chose to push again from the brakeman position, and I chose to as well. Although I did not improve my brake push time, I was very satisfied with my numbers nonetheless. The coaching staff added the total time, brake push plus side push, and the lowest time won. The ranking is similar to how golf is ranked, where the lower the time you post, the higher you move in the standings. The final push championship results were as follows:

1) Chris Fogt – 9.97

2) Steven Langton – 10.01

3) Abe Morlu – 10.22

t-4) Nathan Webber – 10.24

t-4) Curt Tomasvevicz – 10.24

t-4) Johnny Quinn – 10.24

There was a three-way tie for fourth place between Nathan, Curt and myself. The rules dictate that we couldn't leave push championships in a tie, so the coaching staff ranked the three of us to the 100th of a second. That moved Nathan into fourth place with a time of 10.241 seconds, but left Curt and I in a tie for fifth place at 10.247 seconds. In order to break that tie, the coaching staff decided to rank us based on who had the fastest brakeman push. Curt's brake push was 5.09 seconds, while mine was .02 seconds slower at 5.11 seconds, so Curt ended up in fifth place and I ended up in sixth. To be honest, I wish I had won the tiebreaker. Saying I came in fourth place would have sounded better than saying I came in sixth place. Where I did have the advantage over some of the others was in holding the second fastest side push of the event. I knew that if the U.S. only sent two sleds to the Olympics, my push championship performance gave me a strong bias as a side pusher.

The attitude around the locker room had begun to change. Around thirty athletes initially qualified for the combine and push championships, but we were now down to roughly twenty athletes, due to injury or other circumstances. The athletes that tested well and pushed well had a sense of urgency in their step. The athletes that did not test or push well started to lose a little momentum, as the door to their Olympic dreams began shutting.

It's a tough balance when you are in a high-pressure situation like Olympic Trials: clearly, you want to do well, as you are trying to make the team, but you also want your buddies to do well because they are your friends and teammates. During competition it's crucial to understand that you can't take the results personally. Everyone is trying to do their best, and some people score high, while others score low.

We wrapped up our testing in Calgary with a combination push day, in which the coaching staff watches to see how athletes push and interact with other athletes. That may have been my best day. I felt strong competing, and my times in combination with other athletes were fast! I felt like the energizer bunny, like I could just keep going and going and going — or in my case, keep pushing and pushing and pushing. The week in Calgary was over and it was time to head to the Olympic Training Center in Lake Placid, New York. The week after Calgary was used for meetings in preparation for the Olympics and also gave us a chance to continue to push together. There was no snow on the ground in July in Lake Placid, so we pushed our bobsled on wheels. Pushing a wheeled bobsled is decent practice, but nothing can fully duplicate what it's like to push on ice.

With the combine and push championships over, I was eyeing another milestone. I wanted to leave my stamp on the competition and let my coaches and fellow teammates know how serious I was about commanding a spot on the Olympic team. How best to do this? By taking down the power clean record. My buddy and teammate Andreas Drbal set the mark earlier in the year with a monster power clean of 180 kilos (396.8 pounds). Andreas was a former javelin thrower at UCLA and is one of the most powerful guys I have ever met in person. But Andreas was nursing a back injury he had gotten over the summer, so the window was wide open for me to go after the record.

I took my time warming up and started to move into heavy weight. I took a rep at 150 kilos (330.6 pounds) and then moved to 160 kilos (362.7 pounds). The 160 kilos felt heavy, so I knew I needed to shoot for the record fast. I loaded the bar with 175 kilos (385.8 pounds) and smoked the weight. This was the most weight I had ever done in my career. In college, I set the power clean record at 380 pounds, but after blowing out my knee in the CFL, it had taken me years to get back to this kind of strength. A few of the guys in the weight room were hanging around to see if I would go after the record. My successful lift of 175 kilos moved me into second place on the record board, but in my mind, that wasn't good enough. I loaded the bar with 182.5 kilos (401.2 pounds). If I could successfully lift that amount, I would break the power clean record.

I sat on a bench, took a deep breath and visualized completing the lift. I thought about all of my past experiences and everything I had been through that had led me to that moment. I knew God had a plan for my life, even during the lowest of times. As I approached the bar, I prayed silently for God to give me strength.

I set my stance next to the weight just like I had done hundreds, if not thousands, of times before. I took a deep breath, engaged my core and let it RIP! I felt the weight come off the ground relatively fast and as the bar cleared my knee I pulled so hard that I was trying to launch the weight into space! As the weight exploded up, I dropped my hips to catch the weight. I could feel that the weight wanted to fall to the ground, but I wasn't going to let that happen. I powered the weight up to successfully complete the lift and snag the new power clean record at the Olympic Training Center in Lake Placid, NY.

A few of my teammates stayed in the weight room to cheer me on, and we all celebrated after the lift. News spread quickly about the new record, and once the video was posted on social media, everyone in the Olympic Training Center and even bobsledders from other countries were in the know. I was pumped about the new record, but I was also exhausted from all that had transpired that week and the week prior — including the combine, the push championships, the travel and now the power clean record. Although I wanted to celebrate, I knew I needed to nap. So that's what I did after setting the power clean record — I went to my room and took a long nap!

I couldn't have asked for a better start to the Olympic year. We had a six-week break before team trials began. That time off allowed me to go home, see my beautiful fiancée and work to raise sponsorship money for the next season. I headed back to Texas feeling proud of my performance. I knew my goal of being named to the Olympic team hadn't been realized yet, and that the road to getting there was still a long one, but I had gotten off to a very strong start, and for that, I was grateful. The myth that only residents of the Olympic Training Center could make the team was still out there, but it had gotten a lot quieter in recent weeks; helping to quell the buzz was me showing everyone that it was possible to produce at a high level while maintaining precious relationships and working to offset training costs.

Are there any myths in your life that need to be busted? I love what Dr. Covey says in his book *The 7 Habits of Highly Effective People,* where he references pausing between the stimulus and the response. I recommend taking some time to pause and do an evaluation of your life to see what myths are floating around in your head and influencing your decisions. Let's crush those myths!

CHAPTER 25

HANGING ON TO THE DREAM

"It's hard to beat a person who never gives up."

– Babe Ruth

OLYMPIC TRIALS BEGAN in October, just in time for the weather in upstate New York to drop low enough to maintain a solid sheet of ice on the bobsled track. I was heading into team trials with USA-2 pilot Nick Cunningham. Nick is a cowboy from California. He ran track at Boise State and became an Olympian in 2010 as a push athlete for USA-3. After his first Olympics, Nick transitioned to the driver's seat and never looked back.

As a push athlete, you want to be teamed with a driver who used to be a push athlete. Push athletes are constantly ranked on our start times, and to have a driver who understands what a brakeman goes through helps tremendously when pushing the sled. We had two other stud athletes on our sled for team trials. Dallas Robinson, from Kentucky, was the left side pusher. Dallas is a bigger athlete: 6'3" and 230 pounds. He has a track background, and when he's healthy, he can flat out fly. Running brakes for our sled was Abe Morlu. Abe was also a former track athlete who, get this, ran for Liberia in the 2000 Olympics in Sydney, Australia. He was born in Liberia but immigrated to America with his family at age seven, so he had dual citizenship. Abe had already been a summer Olympian, and now he was trying to become a winter Olympian for a different country. Abe finished third at push championships. Our bobsled was loaded with speed — exactly what you wanted on a four-man crew.

Among the other teams, USA-1 was coming off a strong year after winning bronze at the World Championships the previous season. Olympic and World Champion Steven Holcomb piloted the USA-1 crew; the push athletes consisted of Curt Tomasevicz — who won Gold with Holcomb in 2010 — Chris Fogt and Steve Langton. Chris and Steve were on a different crew at the 2010 Olympics that crashed, so they were pushing this time with chips on their shoulders.

The layout for Olympic trials would consist of two parts spanning the month of October. We would spend the first two weeks practicing and competing in Lake Placid, and the following two weeks at the bobsled track in Park City, Utah. The 2002 Olympics were held in Salt Lake City, and we loved practicing, training and competing there because the facilities were nice and new! The start ramp in Park City was built well for sprinters. The drop off is fast, so if you don't have speed the sled will either leave you, or you will have to pull back on the sled to get in, which is a big no-no in sliding sports.

As we prepped for the four-man event in Lake Placid, we continued to keep an eye on the weather. It was a particularly warm October that year, and there were rumors that the four-man trials would be canceled. When you combine the weight of the bobsled with the four athletes, you're looking at a combined heft of around 1,300 pounds. In order for a track to withstand that kind of weight, the ice needs to be rock solid, and the weather needs to cooperate. If it's just ten degrees too warm, the ice will start to melt off the track and the athletes can get injured. We kept hearing rumors that if the weather continued to hold at higher temperatures, we would have to run back-to-back races in Park City, Utah. The rumors turned out to be true, and now the stakes would be even higher in Park City with both of the four-man races.

We braced for the challenge and arrived in Park City, Utah, ready to rock and roll. The four-man race had a lot riding on it, and we were ready. Throughout the week, we pushed well in practice in anticipation for race-day weekend. The night before the race we prepped the sled and made sure it was in pristine condition. In bobsled, we have runners that need to be polished for race day. In order to polish these steel runners, we must use different grades of sandpaper to rub all the nicks and scratches out. Sanding runners can be extremely monotonous and a pain because it takes a good chunk of time. You have to start with high grit sandpaper and work your way down all the varying grits until you finally reach a polishing cloth. Once the runners are fully sanded, they look magnificent. You can see your reflection in the runners; that's how shiny they look after being prepped for the race.

Arriving at the track on race day was special. This was my first time competing at Olympic Trials, and a sense of patriotic pride was flowing through my veins. I was in the process of making my dream a reality, one push at a time. We knew it would be tough chasing down USA-1, but we still gave it our best. We blasted the sled off the top of the hill and our load was smooth. Park City is a shorter track than Lake Placid, with it taking around 50 seconds to complete the course. We pushed fast and we rode fast, but we still came up just a hair shy of USA-1. We finished second at the Olympic Trials on both race days. We felt good about that, but not great. In any competition, whether it's football, bobsled or video games, I compete to win. We came up short but made a strong push towards a spot on the Olympic Team.

The following day our coaching staff held a meeting to announce the U.S. National Team. The National Team is named every year. This is the team that goes on the World Cup Circuit and, every four years, rosters the U.S. Olympic Team. That being said, not all U.S. National Team members make the U.S. Olympic Team. There is really only one guarantee here: if you are not a member of the U.S. National Team, there is zero chance of you making the U.S. Olympic Team.

I felt pretty confident that I was going to be selected to the U.S. National Team after my combine, push championships and Olympic Trial finishes. That being said, in professional sports there really is no such thing as a sure thing. The coaching staff named three sleds to the U.S. National Team, which consisted of twelve guys and two alternates. I was one of the athletes selected and would be starting the year off on the USA-2 sled. I was thrilled.

The selection process is always a tough part of the year. The guys who don't make the team get sent home or put on the developmental circuit. In other words, their dreams of becoming Olympians are over, at least for that particular four-year cycle. Jesse Beckom, a good friend of mine who was also a former college football player, didn't make the team. Jesse and I hit it off early in my bobsled career. I feel like we were cut from the same stone, that we were brothers from different mothers. Jesse had been in the sport for over ten years, and this was his last time to make a run at the Olympic team. My heart hurt for my fellow teammate and more importantly, my friend.

The U.S. National Team packed up and headed back to Calgary to begin the World Cup Circuit. The first three races would keep us in North America before we headed to Europe. Our coaching staff decided to play musical chairs with the USA-2 and USA-3 sleds. They wanted to evaluate different crews to see different push times and how well teams gelled with each other. When we got to the third world cup in Lake Placid, New York, I was told that I would be off of the four-man team that week. I would only be pushing the two-man sled in the Lake Placid World Cup. I knew that it was only a matter of time before it was my turn to sit out, but I was upset that my turn was happening at our home track. Lake Placid was the track every push athlete on the U.S. team had the most experience on. I was worried that missing out on competing on a track I was comfortable with would play against me on push times.

I did my best to block out the distraction of being off the four-man team that week, and instead changed my focus to the two-man race. I pushed the two-man sled pretty well in Lake Placid and thought to myself, *Well, now's as good a time as any to win my first World Cup Medal!* It turned out that the two-man race day was the best day in U.S. Men's Bobsled history. Not only did I win my first World Cup Medal with a silver place finish, but USA swept the podium!

Lake Placid World Cup – 2 Man Bobsled – December 13, 2014

- 1st Place: USA's Steven Holcomb and Chris Fogt - 1:50.19

- 2nd Place: USA's Nick Cunningham and Johnny Quinn - 1:50.74
- 3rd Place: USA's Cory Butner and Chuck Berkley - 1:50.85

To see three American flags flying high on the podium was surreal. It was so special to share in this moment with my teammates and be the first U.S. men's crew to sweep a World Cup event. I have to be honest and share with you that at that moment, when the track judge put the silver World Cup medal around my neck, I was visualizing winning an Olympic medal in Sochi. We were one month away from finding out who the Olympic Team members would be, and my resume was starting to look nice!

I had an extra bounce in my step after the two-man finish. Now it was time for the four-man race day. As I sat in the start house waiting for the four-man competition to begin, I had a teammate of mine who was also "sitting out" that race ask me an interesting question. He quipped, "Johnny, are you prepared not to make the Olympic team?" I pondered his question, as I wasn't sure I heard him correctly. After all, it was a double negative. I thought, *Did he just ask me what I think he did? Does he want to know if I'm preparing myself for the possibility of not making the team?* I said, "No, actually. It has never crossed my mind. I'm only thinking about and preparing to make the team." I waited in anticipation for his response. He said, "Well, I'm prepared not to make the team. Who knows how it will play out this next month, but I am prepared if I don't make it." At that moment, I knew that he was beat. I knew that kind of mindset would destroy you every time. I couldn't imagine putting in all the work to make the Olympic team and then waste valuable time thinking about why it wouldn't happen or why I wouldn't make it. I had no interest in preparing myself for failure.

Henry Ford said it this way, "Whether you think you can or whether you think you can't, you're right." The kind of mindset you bring to a challenge matters. I learned early in life to approach a challenge of any size with a positive mindset. Think the best and then go make it happen!

The reality is, a lot of things are out of our control. What's not out of our control is our attitude and the perspective we can take in any situation. My experience has taught me to approach challenging situations with a positive attitude. I take time to think visually about particular solutions that I would like to see take place during tough times. Whether they happen the way I visualized or not, I know my efforts both mentally and physically were pointed in the directions I wanted to go.

USA-1 crushed the four-man competition in Lake Placid and won gold. They had been on a roll all year, winning gold in the two-man and four-man events at every stop in North America. They were the early favorites for winning the Olympic gold in Sochi in just a few months. USA-2 and USA-3 didn't fare as well in the four-man competition. Because of that, no one knew what the coaching staff had in mind for the next roster move. Everyone had a few weeks to ponder the roster options as we all went home for Christmas Break.

It was so good to be home for Christmas. Returning to Texas for a mid-season break felt incredible. Getting to spend time with my fiancée, family and friends really rejuvenated me. Amanda even surprised me by decorating our Christmas tree in Red, White and Blue. Our entire place was decorated in an Olympic Christmas theme! It was awesome. The time home was just what I needed. The atmosphere with all my family was nice and light before I left for Europe and prepared for the Olympic Team to be named.

We spent the New Year in Munich, Germany, before making the short drive to Winterberg for the start of the second half of the season. Now that we were back in Winterberg, after my mishap during the previous season, you better believe my teammates were constantly checking to make sure that I didn't have an extra set of keys. I sure was glad my double drive escapade from Winterberg to La Plagne and back was over and done with.

I received notice that I was back on the USA-2 four-man sled but with a change in crew. Nick was still our driver, but the coaches put Justin Olson in as the left side push athlete. Justin is a beast of an athlete. He was on Steve Holcomb's 2010 Olympic sled, which won gold. Justin had been nursing some injuries that kept him off of USA-1. I knew he had to be disappointed about that. I was slated to push from the right-hand side and Dallas Robinson would be running the brakes. We had a heavy sled as

Justin weighed around 240 pounds and Dallas was around 235 pounds. I came in at 220 pounds. Thankfully, Nick was a smaller driver weighing in at 200 pounds. Had Nick been in the 230-pound range, we would have all had to go on an immediate diet in order to qualify as a four-man crew. In a perfect world, each crew member would weigh 231 pounds to reach the maximum weight for a sled. Since everyone is built differently, sometimes crews are put together strictly based on how much each person weighs.

We took our first practice repetition as a team early in the week, and the run went well. The sled went flying off the start block, and we were pushing fast. We all agreed to push even harder on the second repetition. So, we did just that, and loaded in smoothly. About halfway down the track on rep number two, it started to get a bit bumpy. When you start feeling bumps in the bobsled, you know something is going on up front, and it usually isn't anything good. Shortly after the first couple of bumps, the sled flipped over and we were cruising upside down, dragging our heads and shoulders on the ice at eighty miles an hour. It was terrifying. But then the sled miraculously flipped back upright on all fours, and we finished through the final curve. We were all shaken up by what had just happened and thinking about how much it hurt. We did not want to crash again.

Thankfully, we travel with engineers, so when crashes occur, or sleds break down for various reasons, we have knowledgeable staff on the road with us to fix everything properly. They took a look at the sled, and determined that there wasn't too much damage. All we needed was an alignment check. Anytime you crash during practice, it is crucial to get back out there the next day and blast the sled off the line just like nothing happened. It helps build back confidence in the driver and crew heading into race weekend. Nick did just that — he had an excellent drive the following day in practice, and we were back on track for a strong performance in Winterberg. According to our practice push times, we were going to be a top contender at the start block on race day.

Warming up in Europe is different than warming up in North America. Most of the roads in North America are flat and spacious, making it easy for multiple athletes to warm up properly at the same time. In Europe though, many of the roads are windy and narrow. It's common to see rookie athletes from other countries sprint around a corner and run into an opponent by accident. It takes a little bit of getting used to — warming up in a different country and dealing with the roads around the bobsled track.

All of the previous seasons that I was in Winterberg it had snowed. But on this weekend's race day, to my surprise, it was sunny and cold. This was a perfect combination for fast ice, which translates into fast start times. It also means faster speeds that often result in more crashes.

We powered the sled off the hill in unison and with speed. Our load was fast, and we sat down in rhythm. Yes, yes, I know what you're thinking. Go ahead; you can chant it, "Feel the rhythm! Feel the rhyme! Get on up, it's bobsled time!" Okay now that we got that out of the way, back to business. We crossed the finish line in the middle of the pack and were waiting to hear our start time. We posted a start time of 5.06 seconds and were tied for fourth overall. Just as important, USA-1, who had been putting a beat down on everyone at the start, pushed 5.04 seconds in the first heat.

We knew the coaching staff was evaluating push crews to see which combination would give USA-1 a run for their money. Let's just say we were fired up after seeing our start time. As we prepared for the second and final run, we knew that we needed another monster start. We delivered all the power we could generate off the starting block into the sled. It shot us out fast, and we were off to the races. The load was smooth and we hunkered down in the sled to get out of the wind. I knew our start was fast. And then it started to get bumpy. *Uh-oh,* I thought, and just like that, *wham,* our sled flipped over, and we were back on our heads in Winterberg. As I tried to protect my head from skidding on the ice at eighty miles an hour, I thought to myself, *this sucks, our push time better be fast!* We finally came to a stop, and the track crew helped us off the track and pushed our sled safely to the finish dock. The medical doctors wanted to check us for concussions, but we were more concerned about our start time. I saw the board first and it read 5.06 seconds! Our crew was ecstatic. This confused the medical doctors because normally after a crash the crew is upset and visibly shaken. Not us, we were almost the exact opposite. We were all incredibly pleased with our start time. USA-1 then went on to smash another powerful start, at 5.03 seconds.

Our next stop was to my favorite bobsled track in the world: St. Moritz, Switzerland! It also marked the two-week mark until the U.S. Olympic Team was announced. I received word that the coaching staff was going to keep our sled the same, with Nick driving, Justin on the left, me on the right and Dallas running brakes. We knew we must have done something right if the coaching staff was keeping us together. We had another strong week of practice together — pushing, working on our timing and loading into the sled.

Unfortunately, USA-3 didn't fare as well in practice that week. They had a serious crash in the four-man sled. It was so bad, their driver had a concussion from it, and he chose to sit out of the four-man race that weekend. You can image how displeased their crew was with the news that they wouldn't be competing that weekend. As race day approached, the excitement continued to build with our team. After seeing the World Cup rankings, we had a chance to secure our spot on the Olympic Team one week early, right there in St. Moritz, Switzerland.

St. Moritz has a heated garage where the athletes can warm up during competition. Come to think of it, add that to the list of why it's my favorite track of all time. I warmed up with a sense of urgency knowing that it was the day to secure our spot on the U.S. Olympic Team. We approached the start block like a pack of fierce wolves ready to devour the competition. St. Moritz is one of the fastest tracks in the world and also one of the smoothest since it's an all-natural track. Each year the start ramp is different because the crew makes it out of ice. And because of that, no one knows what a fast start time looks like.

It turns out, the new ramp agreed with us. We pushed a 5.07, which ended up being in the top five push times for that competition. And even more importantly, we tied with USA-1 who also pushed a 5.07. As we exited the bottom of the track to return to the top of the hill for our second and final run, we came across some wonderful news. Our first run had put us in third place! Not only did we have a chance to secure our spot on the Olympic Team, we had a chance to make the podium in St. Moritz. We had positioned ourselves for a fairytale ending to a crazy Olympic season. As I warmed up for the second and final push in Switzerland, my adrenaline was through the roof. Our next run was what I had been dreaming of for four years. This next push would lock in my spot on the Olympic Team!

We blasted the sled off the hill with another blazing time of 5.07 seconds. I could feel the excitement building at the prospect of making the Olympic Team as we bolted down the track towards the finish line. As we came to the bottom portion of the track something felt off — it started to get bumpy in the sled and then, *wham!* I felt a huge hit on the side of my head and then just like that, we were flipped upside down. We rounded two curves on our heads before I felt Dallas get pulled out of the sled. His ejection pulled me back into the brakeman's seat where I gripped the handlebars as tightly as I could so as not to fall out. I could feel the pressure in my forearms building as the sled tried to rip me out the back. Thankfully, I could feel the sled starting to slow down and knew we must be nearing the finish line. As the sled came to a stop, I could hear members of the track crew running towards us. They grabbed onto our sled so we wouldn't slide backwards into the course. I slithered out of the sled and could see the sunlight beaming against the ice.

Disappointment set in immediately as we all knew that we had just given away an amazing opportunity. Our chance to secure our spot on the Olympic Team one week early was dead. Instead, we were disqualified because we had lost a teammate when he was sucked out of the back of the sled. We could see Dallas walking up with his head hanging low. All of us were upset, but thankfully everyone was okay. We only had a few nicks and bruises — nothing too serious that would keep us out of competition the next week.

We headed back to our hotel and packed up our gear to make the short drive to Igls, Austria. This would be the final week of competition before the coaching staff and selection committee named the U.S. Olympic Team. Nick and I were roommates, and as we were walking out of our room to the van to load our gear, we both sat down on some hallway chairs in exhaustion. We were tired, angry, frustrated and mad about what had transpired earlier that day. The rollercoaster of emotions was tough to deal with. At one point in the day, we had felt joy, excitement and anticipation that the chance to achieve our dream was right in front of us. Then it all went downhill, literally and figuratively; disappointment, anger and anxiety set in after giving away such an amazing opportunity.

I had to take a moment and pause to flush through the ample emotions I had felt throughout the day. What I know to be true is that in order to keep moving forward, you have to get up. You may be beaten down, beaten up or disoriented (I was all three) on the objective you are chasing but you must get up. There is power in standing up when you have fallen and putting one foot in front of the other. You set in motion a fierce determination in your mind and in your heart that nothing will deter you from achieving your goal!

We arrived in Igls, Austria with a serious chip on our collective shoulder and only one mission in mind: make the Olympic Team! The previous week in St. Moritz did not go the way we anticipated, but we had another shot. Another piece of good news was that our USA-3 sled was back in action after their driver, Cory, was cleared following his concussion. The bad news was that because they missed a weekend of racing, the Russia-3 sled pulled ahead of them in World Cup points. Russia was so far ahead in points that we knew we would only be taking two sleds to the Olympics: not three. It was imperative for us to push fast, place well and stay ahead of USA-3 to earn our Olympic bid.

Everyone was laser focused that week in practice. We continued to fine-tune our technique and prepare for race day. The Igls four-man race would be held the afternoon of January 19, 2014, and the Olympic Team would be named later that evening, at midnight. One race remained, and all the marbles were up for grabs. It was time to capitalize on the work we had put in over all those months and years and earn our spot. No one was going to derail us from what we set out to accomplish. Our first push that evening was massive. We tied USA-1 with a 5.00-second start. It was the second-fastest start out of all the countries in competition that day. We had a lightning fast down time too, and that put us in fifth place after our first run. USA-3 had a very good start time at 5.04, but they also had a slower down time that placed them out of the top ten going into the final heat.

We had some down time before the second heat began, so I took a quick jog around the start house area to warm up my legs. I also wanted to clear my mind going into the final heat. The view in Igls is incredible. We were in the Austrian Alps looking into Innsbruck, a major city in Austria that hosted the Olympic Games in 1976. I peered over the mountain and gazed into the distance. *The time is now,* I thought to myself. *It is time to make this dream a reality. There are no more chances. The time is now!*

Our team confidently lined up at the starting block. We knew what was hanging in the balance. The challenge didn't scare us; instead, it fueled us to peak performance. We threw every muscle into the push and loaded quickly with another 5.00 start time. Nothing, and I mean nothing, was going to stop us! Unlike St. Moritz, where the second run got bumpy before the crash, this run felt smooth. It felt really smooth. In fact, it was so smooth that we crossed the finish line in fourth place, putting us one step closer to making the U.S. Olympic Team! Dallas was so excited he even forgot to pull the brakes at the finish line! We flew past the braking section and right into the safety barriers. Typically, the driver would be pretty upset at the brakeman for not pulling the brakes in time. However, our driver Nick kindly let it slide as he understood Dallas' excitement. We all celebrated in sheer joy at what we just accomplished. Four years of bobsled and three years of professional football flashed before my eyes. In an instant, I thought to myself, *this moment was worth the struggle of being cut multiple times and rehabbing a blown-out knee. It was all worth it. The race-off that I won last year but then got demoted after, it was all worth it.*

Sometimes life's biggest struggles are what can springboard us into future successes. I couldn't see it at the time, when I was in the middle of my struggles, but knowing that God had a plan for my life kept my heart and attitude in the right place. I soaked up all the emotions with my teammates. We had just made the U.S. Olympic Team! I had just become a United States Olympian! Well, pending the midnight meeting with our coaching staff and selection committee.

I AM A UNITED STATES OLYMPIAN

*"The two most important days in your life are the day
you are born and the day you find out why."*

– Mark Twain

WE GOT BACK to our hotel in Igls, Austria around 8:00 PM, and it was a painful waiting game until midnight. Four hours of hanging around, waiting for the official announcement on the United States Olympic Team. I called Amanda to check in with her, and she was just as excited as I was and was fully confident that I would make the Olympic Team. I spoke to my parents, brother and a few other people, and everyone echoed the same response as they all tuned in for the race (via the internet) and knew the official numbers and results. I took one more look at the criteria that the coaching staff and selection committee used to evaluate each athlete throughout the season. I felt like my numbers stacked up as good as anyone on the team from testing in July to the last push in Igls just a few hours ago.

Nick, Justin, Dallas and I got to the team meeting room a few minutes before midnight. Both the men's and women's bobsled team were in the same room for the official announcement from our coaching staff and selection committee. The room was packed as the clock struck midnight with everyone sitting in anticipation of the announcement. I glanced around the room to see the looks on my teammates' faces — and their body language.

I noticed something interesting: the guys and ladies who had performed strongly throughout the year sat more upright, as if they were anticipating good news, while the teammates who hadn't performed as well slouched in their chairs, bracing for disappointment.

There was no beating around the bush with Darin Steele, CEO of USA Bobsled and Skeleton. He welcomed us, thanked us for our commitment and went right into announcing the team. On the men's side, they announced three drivers and six push athletes. I earnestly watched Darin's body language to see if he was hinting at who made the team and who did not. I couldn't pick up any clues as he stayed to script and began announcing the guys who made it, which included "Johnny Quinn!" To hear my name called from our CEO was so unbelievably rewarding. The thought immediately raced through my mind that I was officially a United States Olympian. I kept my composure out of respect for the athletes who sacrificed so much but who ultimately came up short. I was all too familiar with that feeling. It had only been a few years since I had tried to make it in the NFL and had also sat in a room waiting for my name to be called, to no avail. I knew exactly what it felt like to work so hard but still get sent home, and my heart ached for my teammates who were experiencing that tonight.

I texted my fiancée, parents and brother that it was official, "I'm on the team! Call you after the meeting." The coaching staff and selection committee kindly asked the athletes who didn't make the Olympic Team to please excuse themselves. Once it was just the Olympians in the room, everyone cheered and celebrated! Some people cried, some laughed, some shouted in sheer joy. I did all three! It was officially official: I was on the team! Although it was after midnight in Austria, it was 5:00 PM in Texas, and since word was out about the Olympic Team, interview requests started to pour in immediately.

On the women's side, there were two athletes, Lauren Williams and Lolo Jones, who had been summer Olympians in the past and were now winter Olympians as well. Only a handful of people in the world had ever accomplished that feat before, so they were highly sought after with interview requests. I spoke to a journalist from the *Dallas Morning News*, and he asked how I felt about making the team. I told him it was such a relief and a reward well worth all the struggles that it had taken me to get to that moment. I went on to share how my football background and the mental toughness I had built up after being cut all those times prepared me for that moment. That was the truth!

I didn't sleep very much that night. The sheer excitement of becoming a United States Olympian and talking to all my people back home on the phone was so much fun. I felt like a little kid in a candy shop! I started to receive the kindest messages on social media and in my email inbox, and stayed up reading all the support that was coming in from back home. I was finally able to get a few hours of shut-eye, and when I woke up the next morning, I literally had to pinch myself so I knew it was real and not a dream. We had one more race on the World Cup circuit before heading to Sochi for the Olympic Games. Our last World Cup race was in Konigssee, Germany, and we took it in stride to work on our technique. Admittedly, we were all focused on our exciting road ahead and in full anticipation of Sochi.

Before flying to Sochi, Team USA had team processing in Munich, Germany. Any U.S. Olympian who was going to Sochi had to fly into Munich first to grab their Olympic Gear and Olympic Credentials. Team processing was just like Christmas morning. The gifts kept coming and coming. On the bobsled team, our main sponsors were Nike, Ralph Lauren and Under Armour. We would go to each station and get fitted and set up with the newest, coolest and latest gear and outfits for the Olympics. We were going to be in Sochi for a month, so each company wanted to make sure we had plenty of gear for our four weeks in Russia. AT&T was the mobile wireless sponsor for the Olympics and gave each Olympian the newest phone so we could stay in touch with our family and friends during the Olympics. We were told the phones came with 500 minutes, 500 text messages and 5MB of data. AT&T wanted us to share our Olympic experience on social media using their phones. It was a win-win for every-one. And it only got better from there. Later on, we found out they had upgraded our plans to unlimited minutes, text and data, so the uploading got a little crazy!

Team USA chartered planes to Sochi for our three-hour flight from Munich. Sochi is a summer resort town in Russia that sits right on the Black Sea. The media covered a great deal of confusion around the world as to why a summer resort destination was hosting a Winter Olympics, but that discussion is for another time and place. As we made the descent into Sochi, I gazed out the window and gawked in awe at the Black Sea. It really is black! I remember calling Amanda and telling her how amazing it was to fly into the city and see the water. You can see this line out in the ocean where it just turns to black. Sochi's airport is small, and the Russians did their best to accommodate hundreds of flights that were carrying athletes, coaches, volunteers, fans, staff, family and friends. Anyone that was coming to the Olympics had to fly into Sochi.

Sochi is about 35 kilometers or 22.5 miles north of the Georgia border, which marks the start of the Middle East. There is a mountain range that separates Sochi and another small resort city from Chechnya, which is currently a brewing hotbed of terrorism. One of the main concerns for the Sochi Olympics was safety for the athletes, coaches and Olympic spectators. The media reports prior to Sochi were not reassuring, and some of my teammates chose to keep their families at home. I, on the other hand, had eight people scheduled to fly over to Russia for the Olympics: Amanda and her mom, my parents, my brother, Chad my football teammate from college, and my aunt and uncle. The thought did cross my mind that maybe they should stay back and watch the Olympics safely from home, but it would have really taken away from the whole experience to not have my loved ones there. The Olympics happen over seventeen days, and the four-man bobsled race was scheduled for day sixteen. They weren't coming until the later part of the Olympics, so I told everyone that I would scope everything out ahead of time and make sure everything looked safe before we made the final decision.

As we stepped off the plane, the first person to meet us was a member of the Russian military, who was holding a handheld infrared scanner. Each time someone exited the plane, the military official would scan the person and it would show a diagram of their body heat on his lens. I'm not sure what he was looking for, but that device he was using was pretty cool. I felt like I was in a *James Bond* movie! Once we cleared customs and grabbed our luggage, we headed to the Olympic Village to check-in. We arrived at the Olympic Village that was called the coastal cluster and was located next to the Black Sea. We had to be scanned in and then taken on a bus to the other Olympic Village called the mountain cluster. The mountain cluster was about a 45-minute bus ride into the Caucasus Mountains. Skiers, snowboarders, bobsledders and any other athletes that had to do with mountain sports stayed in the mountain cluster Olympic Village. The sun was out and shining in the coastal cluster, so people were walking around in shorts and t-shirts. And then in the mountain cluster, it was snowing and people were bundled up in snow pants and jackets. It was crazy to see the drastic climate difference a short 45-minute bus ride could make.

The security was very strong and present everywhere you went. The Russian military had bomb-sniffing dogs go around each bus before it left the Olympic Village. They also put tape on the windows and doors of the buses to make sure no one was tampering with the seals. Every time we got on and off of a bus we had to scan our credentials. You couldn't go anywhere without wearing your credentials. The craziest thing we saw was Russian sniper tents in the mountain range. No one was allowed to drive; transportation was by bus, light rail — or if you were approved media you could have a car. If you were a visitor looking to support your country at different events, you had to get spectator credentials to take either gondolas or Olympic buses from venue to venue.

The Russians had built incredible gondolas that covered a serious amount of ground in order to transport people to the different competitions. At the base of each gondola were Russian sniper tents. They were white camo tents designed to blend in with the snow and there were two snipers in each tent. These tents had small slivers cut along the top portion of all four sides of the tent so that they could see everything that was going on outside, while we could barely see them inside. That was unsettling, but it made taking the bus to practice an adventure as we tried to spot these Russian sniper tents. It was like a much scarier, grown-up version of *Where's Waldo?*

Once we got to the bobsled track, the Russians had military personnel guarding the cooling tanks. Because St. Moritz is the only all-natural track in the world, every other track has a cooling system in place to help keep the ice on the track cold. Sochi was no different. The Russians knew these massive cooling systems would be prime targets for terrorism, so they made sure they were protected by armed guards at all times.

Outside of the heavy military presence, everything was pretty straight-forward and what you might have expected when we arrived in Sochi and finally got settled into our rooms in the Olympic Village. We arrived in Sochi a week before opening ceremonies, which were scheduled for February 7th. Our coaching staff got us into town early so that we would have time to get acclimated to a new time zone and a new location. We had been in Europe for the last two months finishing up the World Cup circuit, so it was only a three-hour time change and therefore wasn't too bad. That being said, it was a ten-hour time difference from Texas, which made video calling with Amanda interesting. Her mornings were my evenings, and vice versa.

As the Olympic Ceremonies approached, Nick, Dallas and I spent a lot of time checking out the activities within the villages. There was so much for us to do! We could play video games, pool or ping-pong; we were allowed to ride bikes around the village and that became our most common mode of transportation. The one stipulation was we were required to be in Olympic gear at all times. But that was no big deal, thanks to all our wonderful apparel friends who had supplied us with roughly five suitcases full of Olympic gear. Nike and Ralph Lauren even had apps installed on our phones so we could see different styling options and what to wear for each activity and our schedule for the day. I could log into my Nike app and select "post-practice interview," and it would show me appropriate options of clothing to wear during the interview. It was awesome! For all the ladies out there who grew up in the nineties, Amanda said it reminded her of a new age version of Cher's closet scene from the beginning of the movie *Clueless*.

As a kid growing up watching the Olympics, I knew how special the Opening Ceremonies were as each country makes their entrance into the

Olympic Stadium. Seeing the torch with the Olympic Flame entering the stadium being lit for the whole world to see was memorable even as a kid. Now I was about to participate in Opening Ceremonies firsthand and see the Olympic Flame in real life! One thing you don't see when watching the Opening Ceremonies is the preparation time it takes to get everyone ready. It took us seven hours to get ready to walk in Opening Ceremonies. You read that correctly, seven hours! Granted, we started in the mountain cluster and it took time for Team USA athletes to travel down to the coastal cluster, but still, seven hours is a long time. Buses were running non-stop and you had to be sure not to miss the last bus, otherwise you wouldn't be walking in Opening Ceremonies. Once we finally arrived at the coastal cluster, we had to use our Ralph Lauren apps that told us how to wear our Opening Ceremonies gear. Ralph Lauren even sent their brand representatives to travel with us and make sure we were wearing their clothing properly. If we didn't have the gear on correctly, we would not be allowed to walk until it was fixed. They were sticklers about the details. Even our shoelaces had to be wrapped twice around the top and tied in the back. The styling was on an all-new level, and something I had never seen before.

Once everyone got dressed, it was time to walk over to the Olympic stadium. That walk gave us a taste of what was to come as Olympic fans lining the streets cheered us on, just as the fans inside the stadium would do a few hours later. When we arrived at the stadium, we were instructed to get in alphabetical order according to country name. I started walking towards the back of the line since the "U" in United States is towards the end of the alphabet. But as I walked, I saw athletes from countries that clearly should have been in front of us alphabetically instead heading to the back of the line. It was the strangest thing! I asked one of the officials where the United States lined up, and he pointed back toward the direction I had just walked from. He then informed me that we were supposed to line up in alphabetical order according to the home country's alphabet, which put us towards the middle. I could now see why this was a seven-hour adventure. No one besides the Russians knew their alphabet, so lining up was interesting, to say the least!

We searched around the stadium for Team USA's standing position and could hear the anticipation from the crowd seated inside the stadium! It was like nothing I had ever heard before — more joyful and frenetic than at any football game I'd ever played at. As the time to march approached, everyone put their phones on record to capture the moment from their vantage point. This was about to be truly a once-in-a-lifetime moment — walking in to the opening ceremonies. We zigzagged back and forth following the signs to the entrance, and as we approached the stadium entrance from underneath, I heard the announcer say: "The United States of America!" I was so filled with pride for my country that hearing him say the name sent chills up my spine and almost brought me to tears. At that moment, we appeared through the entrance ramp and into Olympic stadium for the very first time. A few of the bobsledders stayed close to the front, and I was one of them. I surveyed the entire crowd in amazement, seeing all the camera flashes going off in every direction. It looked like the whole crowd was sparkling!

It was a surreal moment for me, to be walking in Opening Ceremonies and taking in the atmosphere of this once-in-a-lifetime experience. It made all my previous struggles feel worthwhile. At age 26, my dream was over: my football career was a train wreck. But now at age 30, at an age that in the world of professional athletes is considered to be "too old," here I was, a United States Olympian walking in Opening Ceremonies. To wear the Red, White and Blue and be a small part of the 230-athlete delegation sent to represent the United States on the world's greatest stage athletically was incredible! It was a night I will remember for the rest of my life.

Little did I know then that I would also remember the *next day* for the rest of my life. If you recall from Chapter One, the day after the Opening Ceremonies was the day that I got stuck in my bathroom. From that day forward, I would be known as the Olympic bobsledder who had to break down his bathroom door at the Olympics in Sochi, Russia. We had a team interview with Lester Holt of NBC on the afternoon right after the incident. It was my first interview after breaking out of the bathroom. Holt initially focused on bobsled and what it was like to be at the Olympics, before transitioning quickly to the door.

As a matter of fact, all I did for the next few days were interviews with various news outlets who wanted to talk about the door. It became something of a media frenzy: everyone wanted to talk about the crazy door. Thankfully the bobsled race wasn't for another two and half weeks because I had a full schedule of interviews to get through! NBC was one of the first news organizations to reach out. They brought me into their studios and recreated a door for me to break down and to give my three tips on *how to break down a bathroom door.* Matt Gutman with ABC News also recreated a door for me to break out of while yelling, "Good Morning America!" It was awesome seeing that as the morning introduction to Good Morning America the following day.

The media was having a lot of fun with the door fiasco and began to reach out to my family for interviews. WFAA, Dallas-Fort Worth's ABC affiliate, even invited Amanda to be their co-host on the show one morning during the Olympics. Who knew that the power of social media would create such a buzz over a broken door in Russia? I even started to receive memes from people on social media showing how they were "Quinning" out of a situation. Anything that stood in their way, they would break it down and call it "Quinning." I have to admit, people got very creative with their "Quinning" activities, and it made for some good laughs.

A few days after the door debacle, I was heading to dinner with my bobsled driver Nick and one of our engineers from BMW, David Cripps. We took the elevator to the first floor and as the elevator door began to open, it didn't get more than a foot open before it slammed shut again. We all looked at each other in amazement and couldn't believe what was happening. I thought to myself, *you've got to be kidding me, this can't be happening again.* Luckily, we were on the first floor where everyone in the lobby could see what was going on. We also had our phones so we were able to call other Team USA members and ask for help. This was a much shorter stay in a tight space. It was only about ten minutes before a service staff was able to open the elevator doors and let us out.

The jokes were already rolling on in, "Don't go to the bathroom or take an elevator with Johnny Quinn. He seems to get stuck everywhere." Piers Morgan of CNN brought me on his show to discuss all the Olympic

Village mishaps I seemed to be running into at the Sochi Olympics. I told him it had been an interesting few days after Opening Ceremonies, and that no matter where I got stuck, I was going to be ready for competition on race day! Everyone around the world was getting a good laugh from my door and elevator incident. I even received word that people were betting on where I would get stuck next in the Olympic Village.

As I continued to field interview requests from media outlets across the world, it was imperative that I kept my focus on the task ahead. Anytime you compete in a new country or new location, it's important to familiarize yourself with the track and race schedule. I learned over the years of competing that you want your daily schedule to mimic what you will be doing on race day. During the previous four years, it was common for the four-man bobsled race to be held in the mornings. Every now and then, we would have an afternoon race, but most four-man competitions were morning races. When we received the bobsled schedule for the Olympics, the first thing I noticed was the time of the race. Day one of the bobsled race would begin at 8:00 PM, with the second heat starting at 9:30 PM. Bobsled racing for day two would begin in the late morning. In an effort to condition my body and prepare for the evening race time, I made sure to coordinate a few of my workouts between 7:00 PM and 10:00 PM. There was no way I was going to show up to the most important race of my life and not be 100% prepared. It may seem like a trivial thing to switch up practice times, and in the big picture it probably is a small thing, but small things lead to big things — and big things get you beat! When something is important to you, you figure out quickly where you need to be flexible and where you need to stand your ground in order to achieve your dream. Sometimes this requires you to exchange comfortable for uncomfortable. But then again, nobody ever said that accomplishing your dream was going to be easy!

Since the bobsled race was at the end of the Olympics, it gave us time to visit other Olympic venues and watch other Team USA athletes compete for medals. One of the first events we went to was the men's half-pipe snowboarding event. Shaun White had won gold in 2006 and in 2010. He was going for his third gold medal. The excitement in the crowd was building and American Flags were flying high in the stands as Shaun worked to make history! We were standing at the bottom of the half-pipe in the athlete section while the snowboards were getting some serious airtime on the half-pipe. Shaun put together two solid runs, but came up short and missed the medal stand, finishing in fourth place.

Every time we watched Team USA athletes compete, it added fuel to our fire. We saw downhill skiing, speed skating, curling, hockey and more. If there was an opening in our schedule in-between practices, we tried to use that time to "rest our feet" at a venue supporting other Team USA teammates.

Before the four-man race, we had the two-man race. I was not scheduled to compete in the two-man competition, but was selected as the race alternate. In any competition, you must have an alternate ready to fill in if someone gets hurt or gets sick. Ask any athlete: no one really likes being the alternate. You have to do a full race warm-up and 99% of the time, you don't fill in for anyone. There is always that off chance something happens and the alternate has to step in, but for the most part, it's all for naught.

For the Olympics though, it was a different story. It was imperative to have an alternate warmed up and ready just in case. I truly felt honored to be selected as the two-man alternate and I took the warm-up just as seriously as if I was racing in the event. I actually used the warm-up as a walk through for the warm-up I would be doing the following week for the four-man race. Anything that I could do to re-create race day and give my body and mind a preview of what was to come was something I took full advantage of. I would be lying if I said I didn't want to get out there and push the two-man. But, thankfully nothing happened to my teammates and I didn't have to step in for the race. As a matter of fact, our USA-1 two-man sled, consisting of Steve Holcomb and Steve Langton, won the bronze medal. It was so awesome to see them win, and I felt so proud of my teammates! To watch Steve and Steve accept their medals on the podium and wear their Olympic gear was an incredible experience. They brought the medals back to the Olympic Village where we could all see and touch them in real life. It was like adult show-and-tell. Holding that medal in my hand confirmed my desire for my own medal.

Now that the two-man race was over, our team could focus exclusively on the four-man event. My family arrived at the beginning of four-man week, so they were able to catch some of the practice runs and see my crew before race day. It was quite the travel time for Amanda and others coming from Texas. They flew from Dallas, Texas, to New York, New York, to Munich, Germany, to St. Petersburg, Russia, to Sochi, Russia. Two days of travel and a ten-hour time change had everyone ready for a nap! I was able to get passes for everyone for all eight of them to tour the Olympic Village and see our accommodations. One of the cool things about the Olympics is that each sport and country has their own unique pin. It's customary to trade pins with other countries, other fans, or even other teammates within Team USA. A popular pin everyone was trying to get was the Jamaican Bobsled pin. The Jamaican team only had a handful of the bobsled pins, which made them in even-hotter demand.

The interviews were still flooding in from all around the world to discuss the door, but I had to put them on the backburner as the four-man race approached. Lying in bed the night before the four-man race, it finally hit me how special of a moment the next day would be as I stood at the starting blocks. It had been just four short years previously that my dream seemed like it was dead — my football career over. I laid in my bed thanking God for making a new way for me to compete athletically, and thinking about what an honor it was going to be to compete in the Olympics the next day. I normally don't sleep well the night before a competition, but that night I slept like a rock!

CHAPTER 27

IT'S TIME TO PUSH!

WHENEVER IT'S RACE day, I try to keep my emotions in check. I always visualize what I want to do in the race, how I want to push and how I want to load into the bobsled. I went through the same routine that race day too. I ate just enough to fuel my body and made sure to stay off my feet since the four-man didn't start until 8:00 PM. I caught an early shuttle over to the track because I don't like to be rushed in my race-day preparations. Over the years I have found that getting to the track, or in football, the stadium, early on competition day actually calms me down and gets my mind in the right place. I liked the ritual of putting my bag in my locker and walking to the start block to admire the ice. I liked to see how the grooves were cut and then to stare into the stands visualizing what it would look like in a few hours with fans screaming and cheering for their country.

I warmed up the way I always do for a race: taking my time and stretching every muscle. It's my own mental checklist that lets my body know it's about to be "go time!" I could see the fans pouring into the stands, which added excitement to the atmosphere. I kept going over to the railing periodically to search for my fiancée and family. I think the third time I looked, I finally found them and gave them a gigantic wave! I was so glad that my family decided to make the trip halfway around the world for my Olympic debut!

I saw we were fifteen minutes away from the start of the race and that it was time to put on my speed suit. Under Armour designed our Olympic speed suits, and they looked sharp. They were all black with flashes of Red, White and Blue and a gigantic USA down the back of the suit. As I zipped up my speed suit and put on my race spikes, my adrenaline began to rise. I grabbed my gear and rounded up the guys for a quick team prayer. We prayed for strength, safety and healthy competition, and thanked God for the opportunity that had been provided to us.

I put my helmet on and walked the single flight of stairs that led to the start area. I took a deep breath after stepping outside and felt the cold air enter my lungs. My teammates and I all quickly went through a stretch routine to make sure we were all loose. The coach who was helping to load the sled onto the ice motioned for us to come over. That was it. We were up next. Walking to the starting block at my first Olympic Games was so incredible. Standing there with my three teammates ready to blast our sled off the hill in the Olympics is a feeling and moment I will never forget.

I took a quick glance at Amanda, who was cheering abundantly with my family and the rest of the Team USA fans. I grabbed my push bar, locking in my left hand and then my right hand. I breathed calmly, waiting for Nick to begin the start call.

– Nick: "Front Set"

– Dallas: "Back Set"

– Nick, Dallas, Justin, Me: "Ready!"

PUSH! PUSH! PUSH!

As we all said ready, we fell into the sled and exploded off the block together. When all four athletes hit the bobsled at the same time, it literally flies out of the start like a rocket. We crushed the bobsled, and it was time to apply maximum force to the ice, which in turn would translate to speed for our sled. Each step I took was with power and intention. I gripped down hard on my mouthpiece making sure every ounce of effort was applied into the bobsled. We started to pick up speed quickly, and I knew it was time to load in. We had done it so many times it was like clockwork now. Nick would get in the bobsled first and trigger the load. Justin would then take two steps after Nick loaded, and get in. Justin triggered the load time for Dallas and I. When we saw Justin load, that was my cue to take four steps while Dallas takes five steps. Dallas and I essentially come off the ice together and we all load into the sled. There really is quite a bit of choreography and rhythm to it. Nick's legs and feet shoot toward the front of the sled so he doesn't have to worry about sitting on anyone. As for Justin, once he loads in the sled, he has to elevate himself, leaving me room to shoot my legs under and around him, while Dallas shoots his legs under and around me. When done correctly, it looks like poetry on ice. Of all the loading into bobsleds I performed over a four-year span, the load Nick, Justin, Dallas and I completed in the Olympics was by far the best — it was perfect. Everyone was smooth off the ice and got their legs properly into position.

We flew down the ice and I could hear the screaming of fans along the open portions of the track. The fans that weren't able to get a ticket at the start ramp would scatter throughout the track and root us on, as bobsleds would fly by going 80+ MPH. When you're going that fast, you can hear people screaming and cheering, but it mainly sounds like a blur. We crossed the finish line, and I could hear a roar from the fans at the finish block. The Russians brought in extra seating to accommodate spectators where the bobsled would finish. The atmosphere at both the start and finish was amazing. To see the Olympic rings and flags of every country that was competing flying in the air was incredible, making an already amazing moment truly memorable.

We didn't finish as high as we hoped after day one of competition, and our start times began to fall off. We pushed 4.81 on our first start and fell back two-hundredths of a second to 4.83 on second run. It was frustrating to see an increase in start time because the natural progression was to drop time, not add time. We knew we had some work to do and were ready to battle back on day two.

Our USA-1 sled was sitting in medal contention after the first night of competition, and we wanted to do our best to join them. This was the final day of competition and also the last day of the Olympics. Closing Ceremonies would be later that night.

I made sure to arrive early to the track on day two. The time spent alone before competition always put my mind in the right spot to compete. But I was also there early for reasons that had nothing to do with the race that day. I also wanted to be sure and grab dirt from Sochi and put it in a plastic bag. Sounds weird, right? Well, Amanda and I had been engaged for nine months at this point, and we decided we wanted to do an earth mixing ceremony at our wedding. Amanda would gather dirt from where she grew up, where she went to college and other significant places in her life. I would do the same. Since we met three weeks before my bobsledding career began, and she was such a trooper to follow me around the world, we agreed that I would gather dirt from different locations that I competed in during that year. I had gathered dirt from Germany, Switzerland, Italy, France and now Russia. At our wedding we would do the unity portion, lead by our pastor, as we combined earth from all the places we had been throughout our lives, commemorating the separate paths that had led us together. We have our combined earth in a special jar in our house with a map of all the places we collected dirt from across the world!

I made sure to grab plenty of dirt and put it in my bag so I wouldn't forget. I snapped back into competition mode and began to go through my pre-race warmup. As I started to warm up, things felt different. My body felt fine, but my mind felt different. Maybe it was because I knew that it could be my only Olympic Games. It could be my last competition as a professional athlete. I thought about all the moments that had led me to that place, and I started to get emotional. But I had to get my emotions in check and stay on track with my warmup to make sure I would be ready to blast it off the hill for day two of Olympic competition.

The same feeling rushed over me as we stepped onto the start ramp to begin our first run of day two. It was time to rocket the bobsled off the line with the guys I trusted. We dialed in our cadence and pushed with all the might our bodies would allow. Amanda and the rest of my family decided to sit at the finish line for day two of competition. As we came up the finish ramp for the last run, it was so special to have the people I cared the most about at the biggest competition of my life! We got out of the bobsled and I gave Nick, Justin and Dallas each a big hug. It had been an honor competing in the Olympic Games with these guys, and I was privileged to call them my teammates!

We hung around the finish block to cheer on and support USA-1 as they crossed the finish line with a bronze medal. We were so proud of them, and it was great to get an American Flag on the podium! Our crew missed the podium by 1.8 seconds, which put us in 11th place. The result was not what any of us wanted, but that's the reality with competition. Sometimes you win, sometimes you don't. Although 1.8 seconds does not seem like a lot of time, in the sport of bobsled, it is an eternity.

As much as we all wanted to stay and celebrate, including our USA-1 crew, we had to get dressed and ready for Closing Ceremonies, which would begin in a few hours. If it was anything like Opening Ceremonies, we were already running behind!

In Opening Ceremonies, everyone walks into Olympic Stadium with the athletes from their country. It is such a proud moment to be with your fellow countrymen as they announce your nation entering Olympic stadium. Closing ceremonies works a bit differently. This time around everyone walks in together. It doesn't matter who you're standing by, you walk in and sit down as a big group collectively. The Olympic movement wants to promote peace throughout the world, and so the Closing Ceremonies demonstrates all the countries coming together and walking in unity together.

I walked into Closing Ceremonies with an Alpine skier from Argentina on my left and a coach from Kazakhstan on my right. We shared stories about our families, our teammates and where we were from. We laughed as each of us tried to understand one another over obvious language barriers. The Russians put on another amazing show in Olympic Stadium. The Olympic flame was extinguished, which signaled the closing of the Olympic Games. The next time the Olympic flame would be lit would be in preparation for the 2016 Summer Olympics in Rio de Janeiro, Brazil.

The Sochi Olympics were the most expensive Olympics to date, with the cost topping out at over $51 billion. I think they spent $1 billion alone on the Closing Ceremonies firework show. This firework show was essentially a 30-minute finale consisting of the most explosive fireworks I have ever seen. It was the perfect closing to such a special time that I truly will never forget!

I met everyone at the airport the next day. We were planning on taking our time to get back to Texas. We stopped in St. Petersburg, Russia for a night and visited some local attractions before heading on to Munich, Germany. We had a short layover in Munich in order to catch our flight to New York City. We then spent a few days in New York City visiting Amanda's brother and his wife. I really like New York City, and would even think about living there. Amanda, on the other hand, considers herself more of a West Coast girl, so splitting the difference and living in Texas works pretty well for us.

We finally made it back to Texas, and Amanda and I and our sweet boxer Scout sat on our couch exhausted from the travel and jetlagged from the ten-hour time change. I said, "Sweetheart that was fun, and I am so glad we got to experience that together. Do you want to do it again?"

DID BECOMING AN Olympian change my life? Absolutely! But why is that? It showed me that a major setback on a lifelong dream wasn't the end of the story; it was only the beginning. It was the story I couldn't, and wouldn't, have written for myself, but it was far greater than I could have ever imagined. It showed me that consistently pushing for your dreams may not just be preparing you for success, but preparing you for the life-changing story on the other side of what you see as failure. You may not always see what your willingness to PUSH is setting you up to achieve.

Becoming an Olympian after failing in professional football is proof that you can reach an incredible milestone after a massive failure. My hope is that you will pull lessons from my story to assist you in building your life as you PUSH to achieve your biggest and wildest dreams!

It has been quite the ride since returning home from the Olympics. I was a contestant on American Ninja Warrior (ANW), which was so much fun! I did my run during the "ninja-ish" nightfall close to midnight. I ended up falling on the fourth obstacle—the standing swing that needed me to jump to the cargo net. I just missed the net by a few inches. A feeling I knew all too well from the setbacks life had thrown at me. I really wanted to make it to the warped wall. I will continue to push for that dream, and maybe next season I can go all the way!

I had a chance to train with a real S.W.A.T. team. They wanted to show me how to break down a door the right way with a battering ram. They gave me five different battering rams to try out, and I even got to blow up a door with an explosive unit and run a training exercise, which was awesome. Now I know how powerful it can be to have the right equipment with you when you're stuck behind a closed door with no way out but breaking through it.

As a member of the Olympic Team, they flew us to the White House to meet President Obama. Touring the White House was unbelievable. It was so cool to see items from Abraham Lincoln and even George Washington's presidency within the White House. I momentarily debated running for office but decided running a sled was enough for now.

Amanda and I got married at a beautiful venue in Anna, Texas on May 3, 2014. We had our closest family and friends celebrate our special day with an outdoor wedding and indoor reception. We danced the night away, and in perfect competition form, set the new record for most people in a photo booth — cramming 16 people inside a tiny booth. Amanda and I honeymooned in Maui, Hawaii, for a week, and I learned a valuable life-lesson on day one — always listen to your wife! After neglecting her advice to put on sunscreen, I came in from our first day with sun poisoning. Boy did I pay the price for that one!

Shortly after returning from our honeymoon, Amanda gave her two-week notice at work and left her corporate job at a graphic design firm to join me full time. My company, The Athlete Watch, and my speaking engagements were really taking off. As a result, I needed an extra set of hands to help me grow the businesses and help as many young athletes as possible get college scholarships. Amanda and my strengths and weakness complement each other, so working together has been a joy!

I am still training and pushing to stay in shape to try for the 2018 Olympics, but I also recognize I am in a new season of life. Amanda and I both want to have kids one day and settle down as a family. Life on the road and traveling around the world with bobsled would delay our family plan. We are weighing all our options and will move forward with whatever positions us to best achieve our future goals.

Although I don't know what the future holds, I do know who holds the future. He holds your future as well. My hope from this book is that you see God working in my life through all the ups and all the downs. He never abandoned me. Even during times of doubt and low points in my life that I've shared within this book, God had a plan for my life, and he does for you too! What I didn't see coming, was what he had been faithfully preparing me for from the very beginning. What I saw as setbacks were really setups for where He knew I was going to go.

Here is my question for you to consider: What are you going to do with your life? Your life is a gift, and there are people in your realm of influence who are looking up to you. The people you care about the most are counting on you to fulfill your God-given potential. It doesn't matter how many times you have been knocked down, or been counted out. It doesn't matter if you have quit in the past. Today is a new day, and your life can change. There are people counting on you to keep PUSHING, and I know you have what it takes to be that loving spouse, parent, friend or co-worker you were created to be. Who knows, maybe you'll end up becoming an Olympian for the United States of America, too!

You can achieve your dream! You just have to PUSH!

ABOUT THE AUTHOR

Johnny Quinn is a professional speaker who travels the globe to inspire audiences by delivering thought-provoking and action-packed messages to businesses, schools and organizations. A few of his clients include: New York Life, LiftMaster, BMW, Ericsson, Fidelity Investments, American Diabetes Association and Zillow Group.

He is a U.S. Olympian in the sport of bobsled and competed at the 2014 Winter Olympics in Sochi, Russia. Johnny is also a former professional football player spending time with the NFL's Buffalo Bills and Green Bay Packers; he was also a member of the Saskatchewan Roughriders of the CFL. He is one of three people to have played in the NFL and competed in the Winter Olympics. Johnny is the founder of TheAthleteWatch.com, an online pro-active leadership course that helps student-athletes and their families search for scholarships.

Johnny and his lovely wife Amanda (@AmandaQuinnUSA) were married on May 3, 2014 in Anna, TX. They plan on having a family one day!

CONNECT WITH JOHNNY

I met a guy named Bob Goff. He is an incredible human being, and if you haven't read his book "Love Does," please go pick up a copy. It is my #1 favorite book of all-time. Bob talks about following Jesus and what he has learned about being with people just like Jesus was 2,000+ years ago.

Bob mentioned that a lot of people stop being available as time goes on. We either get busy and life happens or we just stop wanting to be available because things get messy. If you look at Jesus' ministry on earth, He loved being with people and would always be available. What a great demonstration of what it looks like to love one another.

As I look at my life, the times that I have grown the most and the times that I needed help the most are when other people were available to me. I want to be available to you if there is anything you would like to chat about. You're welcome to give me a ring on my phone at (972) 658-5540. Call me sometime if there is ever anything I can do for you.

Your friend,

Johnny Quinn, U.S. Olympian

P.S. If you are on social media, I would love to connect with you. My handle is @JohnnyQuinnUSA

CPSIA information can be obtained
at www.ICGtesting.com
Printed in the USA
BVHW03*0045090218
507701BV00001B/4/P